The Growth Trap

Endorsements

This book is like a how-to manual on how to avoid the traps in life personal and professional. It also serves as a handbook on growth. Definitely a must read for any up and coming professional or anyone looking for personal growth.

Hovain, President of Cinematic Management,
Hip Hop music executive manager

Ralph's story is inspiring and relatable to all people. The stories gave me perspective around my own "Growth Trap" Situations and helped me think differently about leveling up in my own industry of work.

Brandon T. Adams, 2X Emmy® Award-Winning Producer,
Host of Success in Your City

I've known Ralph through the last decade, post market crash and I've seen him grow out of the most challenging of situations and rebuild multiple businesses from 0. This book is a testament to how growth can lead you to traps and it shows you how to be aware of them in order to keep being a better version of you.

Anthony Lolli, Author, Business, Fitness and Media Entrepreneur

The Growth Trap is a wonderfully written book by a self-made industry leader who has taken his life's experiences and consolidated them into a masterful read. A must read for anyone who has struggled with both professional and personal issues through-out their lives and careers. A positive take away from every chapter that is sure to help you get the most out of life and what it brings.

Rich Sadiv, Owner Parisi Speed School

My brother has reached great heights, and he is sharing a truly honest account of how that came to fruition so others can do the same. His very personal accounts of the highs and lows are the cherry on top of him now sharing the roadmap he's formulated that others can now follow. From being a tough kid on the streets of Brooklyn, overcoming the pitfalls of the world we grew up in, and then having to get knocked to the mat after early business success and build it all up bigger and better than before. Ralph reveals here how the journey is ongoing, and if you dedicate to not getting caught in the Growth Traps along the way, we can succeed to the highest levels.

Having watched this all from the front row, I can tell you that it is a modest recollection of the boy that always acted like the man. From standing up to everyone (including me) since birth, soaking up the experience and knowledge of those he admired, and outworking everyone as he strived to be the best at whatever he did. Him writing this book came as no surprise, because he's added mentoring to his toolbox, and he's changing lives every day. I can attest to his greatest growth, is that of a leader. And this book is his way of leading you out of your own Growth Traps. I'm sure you'll be as inspired as I was by it!

Michael DiBugnara, Co-founder and CCO of LIKEY

The Growth Trap is a Must-Read for anyone who is looking to achieve growth in their personal and business life and are ready to level up their game. We all experience Growth Traps throughout our careers and this book helps you overcome them.

Kevin Harrington, Inventor of the Infomercial and
Original Shark on ABCs hit show *Shark Tank*

THE
GROWTH
TRAP

A Continuous
Plan to Avoid
the Traps of
Life and Build
a Better You

Ralph DiBugnara

NEW YORK

LONDON • NASHVILLE • MELBOURNE • VANCOUVER

The Growth Trap

A Continuous Plan to Avoid the Traps of Life and Build a Better You

Published in New York, New York, by Morgan James Publishing. Morgan James is a trademark of Morgan James, LLC. www.MorganJamesPublishing.com

Proudly distributed by Ingram Publisher Services.

Morgan James BOGO™

A **FREE** ebook edition is available for you or a friend with the purchase of this print book.

CLEARLY SIGN YOUR NAME ABOVE

Instructions to claim your free ebook edition:
1. Visit MorganJamesBOGO.com
2. Sign your name CLEARLY in the space above
3. Complete the form and submit a photo of this entire page
4. You or your friend can download the ebook to your preferred device

ISBN 9781631959158 paperback
ISBN 9781631959165 ebook
Library of Congress Control Number:
2022934168

Cover & Interior Design by:
Christopher Kirk
www.GFSstudio.com

Morgan James is a proud partner of Habitat for Humanity Peninsula and Greater Williamsburg. Partners in building since 2006.

Get involved today! Visit MorganJamesPublishing.com/giving-back

Dedication

To everyone, who over the last Twenty plus years of my career, who has helped me blindly on this wonderful journey.

My Family, Friends, Colleagues, and Teachers of the lessons I needed to learn.

To My wife Beatriz and children Lucas and Leina. You make it easy for me to get up every morning to work towards a better me and us. I am inspired daily by your support and your confidence that I will do what is right and needed for the future of our family.

To my Father and Mother, Ralph and Joanne. Thank you for letting this curious child find his own way, never trying to change me, loving me, leading me by example, and setting me up to be as successful as I am willing to become.

To My brother Michael and his amazing family. You led the way to try and make my path easier by defending me, backing me up no matter what, and supporting me when I needed it most. You are always in my corner.

There are too many other family and friends to mention but you all have been there for me and are a piece in all I have built and will continue to build in the future.

Acknowledgments

William Arthur Ward, American Motivational writer, wrote "Adversity causes some men to break, others to break records."

As I am finishing writing this book, what I am most proud of is my journey from a kid that was broken by anything to an adult who refuses to be broken by anything. These following people have served as a support system that has enabled me to continue to break my own records and grow from the traps of life. They are in some sort of chronological order but their help has never been limited to a day, month, or year in my life.

To my parents Ralph and Joanne. Your selfless and tireless work when I was a child not only protected me when I didn't know I needed it, but it told me through words and actions that I could be whoever I wanted to be no matter what the rest of the world thought of me. The sacrifices you made so we didn't want or need anything have shaped me into the person I am today for my family. You are the foundation that allowed me to be so strong when I needed it most. My eternal support system that has never wavered.

To my Brother Michael. You were my model in so many ways that set a bar for me to strive for. When we were young, it was your intellect , toughness, and fashion sense that made me want to be just like you. As we got older you showed me that there was no reason we couldn't be whoever we wanted to by being daring enough to step into fields and circles of people that were completely foreign to us. I saw you and realized I could do it as well. Thank you for being there during my darkest times and to cheer the loudest for my wins. Love you, Keily, and the girls very much.

To my cousin Nicky. Our perennial older brother. I've learned so much from you about business and life that I still use in my daily routines to this day. You taught us that nothing was ever unattainable and always told me that I was going to be very special. You believed in me before the world even knew I existed. You, as well as my beloved Aunt, Phyliss, and Uncle Justin, have always been a shining light in my life.

My close knit family and extended brothers and sisters. Cousin Dom, forever my running mate, Vinny, Justin, Aunt Annette and Uncle Paulie, Uncle Mike, Elaine, Cathy, Elizabeth, Patty and my Aunt Genie. Thank you for always bringing happiness and guidance.

To all of my friends and family that were such a huge part of my growth and the best memories a boy who became a man could ask for. Big Mike, Ronnie, Matthew, RJ, Mazzella, Pattie D, and so many more. My childhood is still some of the greatest times of my life, countless laughs and experiences, and we are still together to this day. What we have can never be broken and I wouldn't trade a moment of it for the world.

To Nick Farina, thank you for believing in me when everyone else didn't want to give me a chance. You gave me a window of opportunity that would eventually become my world and I will never forget how you saw something in me for that moment.

To the friends and colleagues who were there for the crash and the rebuilding of it so many times. Sickamore, you showed me that we could create new movements for the world to see and use. Tommy, you have been more than a business partner, but now a brother for the rest of my life. Your strength and fortitude empowers me daily to accept no less than we really deserve. To Frank, for your push and drive to make us all better. You have empowered me to greater heights and shown me how we can be better as a team playing to our strengths. To Jimmy, for your calm guidance from the first day I met you. You have shown sacrifice and the will to move forward when it was needed mosts. Roberto, thank you for backing me up blindly so I could grow as a leader and setting me free when you believed it was time to achieve more. Hovain, you are a constant supporter only for the reason of being a good friend and not for any personal gain. Grateful to be able to watch your growth as a man, father, and businessman. Appreciate you for purely wanting me to win.

To my wife, Beatriz. You have held me up in some of my darkest moments and inspired me in some of yours. People from the outside looking in wouldn't believe that I am mostly a dreamer, but you have never wavered in backing me up on this strange journey. You are an amazing Mom and a constant source of challenges, which I secretly need daily. I fully believe we have, and will continue to, get over whatever obstacles are out in front of us together. Keep being you, you are needed. Love you.

To my children Lucas and Leina. I don't even know where to start explaining to you how much you inspire me and have changed me for the better. Nothing has been as life changing as becoming your father. Something I never knew I wanted but I could never live without. Lucas, you surprise me everyday with your intellect, curiosity, and kindness. I've never had anyone in my life who could so easily walk into a room and make friends immediately without fear and be embraced so lovingly. You are going to change lives one day for the better in whatever you decide to do. Leina, you light up a room with just a look. I can visualize and hear your giggling and witty sarcasm by just closing my eyes. We laugh sometimes just by looking at each other, you may get my sense of humor more than anyone in history. I can't wait to see how you use all of it to impact this world in whatever way you decide you want to do.

A special thanks to all that contributed during and before the process to make this book possible. Eulogio, for your confidence and loyalty to helping me make something great with the beginning and advancement of Disruptors Network, as my brother and ally. Grant, for bringing me to life, visually, in a way I never thought possible. Keyla and Vicky for supporting me in whatever way I have needed to create more. Enmy, Logan, and Failen for your contribution in writing this book.

My name will be on the front cover as the acknowledged author of this book, but the story was created by so many along the way. I live and write most of this story at the moment. The beauty of that is, I won't remember all of the sentiment I put in while I wrote it, but by the next time I write another chapter I will have lived, failed, learned, and grown more for wherever this journey takes me. Here is to welcoming my next growth trap and figuring out how to advance past it and be a better and greater human being.

Foreword

Oftentimes, when requesting someone to write a forward to a book on self-improvement the author chooses some expert in the field or a wordsmith. I am neither of those, but one can appreciate a book of this type regardless of the field you are working in. Ralph DiBugnara is someone who has succeeded despite suffering serious setbacks. He is that rare individual who is never discouraged by failure and in fact as the book avers failure it would appear has made him a stronger individual. One can spend a lifetime reading self-help books and still not be willing to make the individual sacrifices needed to make a "Comeback."

Ralph, frankly, knows of what he speaks and is willing to share that valuable information with others. This writing represents an honest and clearly written assessment of his struggles and triumphs.

Mr. DiBugnara is deserving of much credit for producing a concise and clear path to self-improvement. The author has brought his strict training and "can do" attitude to inspire others. He has not only met his life goal, but he is currently sharing his success by funding a scholarship program for minority students. His mortgage company workforce can serve as an exemplar of diversity.

His work illuminates the idea that each person can achieve their goal if you can learn from your own failures. The idea that "you are the only one that you are competing against "should be the mantra for all who seek to reach their goals.

The author is not only a business success but an accomplished athlete, journalist, and parent. The takeaway here is that you will most assuredly improve your life by following the prescription laid out in the book. One can only predict that we will continue to hear great things from the author.

Ralph DiBugnara, Sr., Father

Table of Contents

Introduction

It's easy to grow when we're children. We get bigger every year, we grow more capable, we jump from grade to grade, and we soak up everything around us. But this only occurs "naturally" up to a point. By the time we're graduating from college or starting our first full-time job, growth no longer comes so easily. If we want to continue to improve and progress in life, we have to be proactive. Failure to consciously take steps toward self-improvement and subsequently getting stuck in life is what I call the *growth trap*.

It's possible to fall into a growth trap in any stage of your life. The growth trap is like pushing a boulder up a hill: in order to prevent the rock from falling, you need to constantly exert effort. The requirement for growing—whether physically, emotionally, financially, or mentally—is the same: you need to expend energy every day to continue to improve. Otherwise, like a boulder on a hillside, you will fall into the pits of a growth trap. Growing is a *proactive* process.

I was very young when I fell into my first growth trap. I grew up in a small Italian community in Brooklyn, in a neighborhood called Dyker Heights. There were only two schools in the entire neighborhood, and everyone knew each other. I was a well-liked kid: very popular, very athletic, and, as a result, very happy. I'd go to the schoolyard and hang out with the older kids whenever I wanted. In the classroom, I did the bare minimum to get by, and it worked for me. My neighborhood was a comfortable cocoon—I never wanted to leave.

When I was thirteen, my parents decided to move from Dyker Heights to Staten Island because our neighborhood was getting worse steadily but surely (I was robbed at knifepoint once). Despite the noticeable deterioration, I still didn't want to leave my beloved home. At our new place in Staten Island, I had to start over. I was no longer liked by girls, no longer M.V.P. of the baseball team. I was forced to make new friends, and I had no idea how to do it. Turned out I was shyer than I'd thought.

I ended up sitting alone in my house for a year. I'd go to school and come back and do absolutely nothing. In eighth grade, I joined the basketball and baseball teams, hoping to get out of my funk. I attended one baseball practice, and I felt so out of place that I never returned. I'd been so good at baseball back in Brooklyn, but after this one moment of insecurity, I never played the sport again. I still kept playing basketball at least, but it was obvious that I was an outsider. The other kids had already been playing together for years, and I could never truly make my way into their circle. Not only did moving cause me to retreat into my shell, but my physical prowess was affected, too. My loss of confidence translated onto the basketball court, where I'd clearly lost a step from my Brooklyn days. While I made the team in Staten Island, I was placed on the bench most of the time. And that only damaged my confidence further.

I was in a growth trap, and I had no idea how to climb out of it.

My identity was completely shaken. I was no longer the cool, fun, popular guy that I'd been in Brooklyn. In Staten Island, I was shy, insecure, and shaken. So who was I, really?

When I was fourteen, my friends from Brooklyn came to visit me. We were walking around, as kids do, and we ended up meeting some other teenagers from the local neighborhood. Because my friends were with me, I had the confidence to speak to the locals in a way that I hadn't had before. It was a shot in the arm for me: I suddenly knew that I *could* make headway in my new home. It felt like coming out of darkness. Suddenly, I looked forward to being outside again, and everything somehow felt new, like I was being reborn. I learned how to be myself again, and I started my growth process. To be sure, my confidence levels still had a long way to go. Girls still made me nervous, and sports were still more difficult than they used to be. But I made progress in getting out of my slump.

My growth trap extended to the classroom, too. In high school, I could no longer get by easily by putting in the minimal effort, which had worked for me back in Brooklyn. Now, I had to study far more just to pass, and I never excelled.

This trend continued when I attended the College of Staten Island (I wasn't accepted anywhere else). All of my friends were away having the classic college experience, while I was still stuck in the same place, literally. I was envious of them, so by my second semester, I wanted to transfer. My plan was to get good enough grades so that I could move away. My motivation was strong enough: eventually, I transferred to the University of Albany.

I chose that school because I had a friend who was already there, and he said that we could live together. I figured that I'd be able to make friends easily, since I'd already have one who would introduce me to people. I'd be able to skip an adaptation period like the one that had been so disastrous back when I moved to Staten Island.

On my first day at the University of Albany, I went to my friend's apartment. He wasn't there! I called him, and he told me that he had to return to his parents' house since he'd failed so many classes that he was forced to drop out. He had neglected to tell me this beforehand. So yet again, I was all alone in a new place.

The college placed me in a suite of three rooms in a college dorm with a bunch of guys who were all in the same fraternity. In my new room, I could immediately see that my roommate was not happy to see me. He told me that his old roommate was coming back, and that I shouldn't have been there.

I didn't want to be where I wasn't wanted, so I went to the administrators and requested a different living arrangement. Luckily, they were able to get me my own room in a different suite with six other guys.

I lasted for about three weeks.

I just wasn't mentally capable of breaking through any of the growth traps still plaguing me. I didn't have the mental fortitude for the social or academic pressures on me. So I quit.

I wanted so badly to return to my parents and Staten Island, and that's what I did. My dad has always been a hardworking guy. He worked three jobs so that my brother and I never wanted for anything. He's the epitome of the "strong, silent" type, so he was never going to tell me how I should live my life. He allowed me to make my own mistakes. This served me well later on in life, but early into adulthood, I was lost. I needed guidance.

I stayed home for the next three or four years, safe and comfortable in my familiar cocoon. The guys I looked up to at this time weren't exactly doing the right things, but they had a lot of money. They were nice to me, but their jobs weren't aboveboard. My friends and I got involved with these people to make some money, because that's what we knew. Selling weed, collecting money for gambling, and similar activities were completely normal to us. And I was looking to prove myself, regardless of the ethics of my decisions. I wasn't interested in breaking out of my comfort zone or becoming a better person. I learned how to survive in this environment, but I didn't expand my mind-set beyond the streets of Staten Island. I was able to fit in with the criminal class, but I did not develop any talents that could elevate me beyond that.

Eventually, I did graduate from college, but it didn't mean anything to me. I didn't walk on the day of graduation, and to this day, I've never picked up my diploma.

My early twenties were some of the most stressful years of my life. I knew that I wanted to be better than where I was in life, but I didn't know what to do about it. The stress got so bad that I developed ulcers.

My childhood in Brooklyn 1990

I began interviewing for jobs, but I was only receiving attention from sales teams—I didn't mind, since I had no idea what I wanted to do. I sold copiers for a little while, and I hated it. Walking door to door in Manhattan and asking people if they needed copier supplies didn't appeal to me. I was gearing up to take a job with Enterprise Rent-a-Car when a friend contacted me with a new opportunity. Thank goodness he did.

My friend, Nick Farina, was in the mortgage business, which was hot at this time in 2001. He told me that I'd go through his company's training program for a month and then jump on the phone for sales calls. I asked Nick what the salary was, and, to my shock, he told me that there *was* no salary. He told me that I'd be paid by commission, but that plenty of people were already making a lot of money doing this.

At that time, Nick was the only person who had any faith that I could make something of myself. Years later, when I reached out to thank him, he said, "Ralph, the cream always rises to the top. You would have made it no matter what." Still, I looked him in the eyes and told him how much I'd needed him back then and how grateful I was that he'd been there for me.

Sometimes, to get out of a growth trap, you have to have your back against the wall. I didn't want to be the guy who lived with his parents and had no job. I didn't want to embarrass my family. I only had a couple thousand dollars in cash to my name. So I gave the opportunity a go, despite my fears.

I started in November 2001. My company was in the Federal Reserve building, near the World Trade Center. Only two months after 9/11, the area looked like a warzone. And that's where my career began.

The office environment was extremely aggressive. Just like in my neighborhood, I had to adapt to the company's culture in order to survive. I'd always been a hard worker, and I always wanted to make money—those were never my issues. At my new job, I worked twelve-hour days and weekends. After a few months, it finally paid off. My first big check was for eight thousand dollars, and the one after that was for twenty thousand. Once I got the feeling that, if I worked hard enough, I could really make a lot of money, my mind-set completely shifted. I *desired* to grow. If I could get really good at this, I could flourish financially.

My job consisted almost entirely of phone sales, which didn't come naturally to me. As a sports fanatic, I'd always been good at studying the stats of my favorite professional athletes. Here in the business world, I leveraged this ability of mine to compensate for my weaknesses. I constantly fed myself information and studied the fundamentals of lending and real estate. It became a daily obsession of mine. I became a dynamic, knowledgeable salesman. To this day, my ability to offer an impressive amount of information to clients has been one of the most pivotal factors in my successful career.

By the end of my first year in the business, I'd made six figures. Within sixteen months of starting my sales job, at twenty-three years old, I bought a house. I'd finally broken through my professional and psychological growth traps.

Growth Traps Come in Many Sizes

I went through an adolescent growth trap, a social growth trap, and a professional growth trap. But you can get stuck in all sorts of other ways. For example, the growth trap can occur in relationships, too. The beginning of a romantic relationship is often very easy. But when you decide to move in together, get married, or have children, it's no longer so simple. Responsibilities, friction, and disagreements inevitably emerge, and you have to work at the relationship every day. During the "honeymoon phase," it's easy to find happiness without trying. After that, though, you need to put the effort in to make the relationship work.

Physical growth traps are also common. Alex Rodriguez was drafted into the MLB at seventeen years old and began to play a year later. He was an absolute phenomenon. He was so naturally gifted that he grew to sky-high levels of performance with ease. Growth came naturally to him. His career consisted of multi-hundred-million-dollar contract after multi-hundred-million-dollar contract. Every year, his stats improved. But, like with any human, his body eventually started to break down. Rodriguez used steroids in order to compensate so that he could penetrate his physical growth trap—he wanted to heal more quickly from his injuries and bolster his batting statistics. Because he'd been so used to effortless improvements, once he found himself unable to grow any further, he lacked the discipline to do the work required for honest growth. Granted, as our bodies age, we simply cannot continue to improve in our athletic abilities. But Rodriguez could still have chosen to optimize his performance in his later years by honorable means. He ended up getting suspended for a year and apologizing to the public (after initially lying about his steroid use).

Rodriguez's trap was physical in nature, but the effects of it were psychological: he compromised his integrity in order to rise from his growth trap. But this ended up destroying him, his career, and his reputation. Later, after growing as a person (ethically and otherwise), he returned to the public spotlight. Luckily, he's turned things around for himself. But not everyone who tries to take the easy road out of the growth trap is so fortunate.

Growth traps are not limited to affecting *people*, either. Entire companies can suffer under a growth trap. At one point, BlackBerry controlled 50 percent of the smartphone market in the United States and 20 percent of the global market. By 2007, the company was pulling in more than three billion dollars in revenue and enjoyed a net income of more than six-hundred million dollars. At some point, the developers at Blackberry approached the executive team and told them that they needed to create a phone with a touchscreen and a web browser in order to compete with Apple's then-new iPhone. The leaders at Blackberry disagreed because they thought that their phones would forever remain the best product on the market: everyone loved Blackberry phones' physical keyboards! Apple and others entered the market, and as everyone now knows, this was the end of Blackberry. It turned out that consumers preferred touchscreens to clunky buttons. In 2013, the company was bought by FairFax Financial at only nine dollars per share.

Blackberry's growth trap was hubris: they thought that they knew better than everyone else how they should proceed. They didn't think they needed to adapt and grow, even while their competitors were advancing around them. A growth trap destroyed Blackberry in only a few years.

Learning to Grow

Since my first sales job, I've gone through a ton of ups and downs, which I'll get into later in the book. Even though that was where I finally broke through my growth trap, it wouldn't be the last one I had to overcome. Now, though, I'm proud to say that I'm flying at a steady altitude in life. As a successful mortgage broker and real estate entrepreneur, I have closed forty billion dollars in career loans, and I have a personal real estate portfolio in excess of fifteen million dollars. In my day-to-day, I also pass on my knowledge of how to be a successful entrepreneur to the next generation of real estate agents. I've made something of myself because I've mastered the art of climbing out of any growth trap that might creep up on me. The following chapters will explain how you can do the same and how you can learn to make incremental improvements in your life every day, both personally and professionally. I'll outline the principles I apply in my own life in order to succeed, and I'll use examples from both my life and others' in order to illustrate how you can do the same. This book is for *anyone* who seeks to make progress, regardless of your age or goals. The growth trap is inevitable. Whether or not you overcome it . . . that's up to you.

Chapter One—

Think Like a Beginner

The Ring

I had to lose my confidence and then regain it in order to believe that there are no limits to what I can accomplish. Sports was my first love and my biggest loss when I fell into the growth trap, as I explained in the Introduction. I had totally lost my confidence on the field and the court. Even today, I look back at my teenage years with regret over what I could have been.

In 2003, as my career was booming, my life started to turn around. This gave me my *mental* confidence back to some degree, and I decided that I needed a physical challenge in order to regain my *physical* confidence. Boxing was always a great love of mine, but I had never learned how to really fight. As a young man growing up in Brooklyn and then Staten Island, I was in plenty of street fights, but those were done in anger. Back then, I fought in order to prove or defend myself. They weren't really skill-based. With those street brawls, I was just learning what to do on the fly. There wasn't a lot of skill involved.

1

But now I decided to learn how to box like a professional.

I found a gym in downtown Manhattan called Trinity Boxing Club. At the time, the sight of the gym was a little eerie, since it was right at the foot of the World Trade Center, overlooking the areas being rebuilt.

Ralph boxing in 2005

The owner and main trainer of the gym was a guy named Martin Snow. He's originally from Brooklyn, and his accent couldn't have been thicker. He's also an imposing figure, standing at around six feet, four inches, and weighing two-hundred-and-fifty pounds. To this day, Martin has long hair and wears a big bandana, shorts, and sleeveless shirts even when it was freezing in the winter. He was also a New York State amateur boxing champion. Recently, he's become famous because he trains one of the women on *Real Housewives of New York*, a popular reality show.

Martin taught me how to box. As my mental confidence steadily returned, along with increasing financial stability, I found that my confidence in my physical abilities also started to come back. I already had some natural ability when it came to boxing, as I had a background in athletics. I'm not proud to say it, but my experience fighting in the streets as a youth actually prepared me for boxing, too. I trained at

Trinity Boxing Club for five or six months, and through sparring and other boxing exercises, I'd gotten really comfortable again. My gym became another homely cocoon—the other guys became my friends, and I never embarrassed myself there. Frankly, I was so comfortable that it almost became another growth trap.

One day, Martin approached me and said, "Hey, we're having a smoker at the gym, and you're fighting." A smoker is an intergym fight. These are amateur boxing matches that used to be very popular in New York City. I had never heard of such a thing before. I told Martin that I wasn't ready for a fight. Martin is the kind of guy who doesn't really ask if you want to do something, he *tells* you that you're going to do it. So he told me that I had to be one-hundred-and-sixty pounds in four weeks, and that he'd see me the night of the fight. I nearly fell to my knees in shock.

A month later, the night of my first fight came. I had no idea whom I was about to fight. Moreover, they match you up based on weight, not experience level. So I figured I was fighting someone far more experienced than me.

I waited downstairs at the gym with nervous anticipation. The worst thing about amateur boxing is that you stand in the locker room, watching people come back bloody and beaten up while you're waiting to enter the ring. I saw maybe seven boxers come back before my own fight began, each looking like they'd been tossed through a meat grinder. This only added to my anxiety.

I'd invited my circle of friends to come watch, including my brother Michael. Three years my senior, Michael was my first role model. As kids, he toughened me up by beating on me all the time. He's always been very proud and protective of me. My dad came, too, though my mom wouldn't come—she couldn't bear to see me get hit. There were about twenty people in total there to watch me.

I finally headed upstairs for my fight. I still didn't know whom I was fighting, all the way up until I entered the ring. There were only about two hundred people there to watch, but it felt like there were five thousand. The guy I fought was a little bigger and taller than me, and he was definitely stronger and more experienced. I remember walking into the ring, but I don't remember what happened after that. Adrenaline took over, and all of my training went out the window. It was a three-round fight, of which I don't recall a single moment.

Ralph and Martin Snow, Trinity Boxing

I won by a razor-thin margin. It felt like I had overcome an unbelievable hurdle, not just in the ring, but in my own mind-set. The victory gave me a new lease on my athletic ability that I enjoy to this very day. That one match led me to continue boxing for the next four or five years.

I fought another fifteen or twenty times. Every time I went to fight someone, I'd still be uncomfortable going into it. But every time I got up there, I acquired a little more confidence. Not only did my physical confidence grow, but it also gave me a new mental ability to get in front of a crowd of strangers and perform. Surprisingly, this helped with public speaking: nothing seemed scary after entering the ring with another man who intended to pummel me! I didn't win every match, but I was definitely good at boxing and won my fair share.

The entire adventure was a huge step in the building of my personal foundation. My experience with boxing was the epitome of losing confidence and then regaining it. I learned that there was really no cap on my abilities and that I had just stopped accessing them during my darker moments. Boxing helped me understand that there was no limit on what I could do, as long as I was willing to put the work in and, more important, get past my fears. Thank goodness that Martin pushed me into fighting against my better judgment. Thanks to him, I learned that I could start at zero and grow over and over again in any domain in my life.

On Top of Her Game

Monica Seles was a famous American tennis player who was once number one in the world. By 1993, the nineteen-year-old had won eight of her last eleven Grand Slam events. On Friday, April 30, 1993, Seles faced off against Magdalena Maleeva in a quarterfinal match in Hamburg, Germany. While sitting on the bench between sets, a crazy fan approached Seles and stabbed her with a nine-inch knife. She suffered a brutal half-inch wound between her spine and shoulder.

Seles lost everything. She had to undergo surgery and therapy before returning to the court. She lost her confidence. During her recovery, she suffered from depression and developed an eating disorder. Despite the traumatic attack, she willed herself back to regaining self-assuredness during her more than two years of recovery. In 1995, she returned to the tennis court and won the first tournament she entered following her absence. Seles went on to win even more Grand Slams. It was an uphill battle, but she eventually worked her way back to becoming the number one player in the world. She was forced into a beginner's mind-set, but she did not let the setback prevent her from progressing back to success.

My Expert Blinders during the Crash

Thinking like an expert has gotten me into trouble more than once. The biggest wakeup call came in 2007. I was cruising along in my career, my income was rising every year without me doing much to grow, and the mortgage market was still getting hotter and hotter. There may have been signs of a crash coming, but I had my expert blinders on, and I didn't see them. I thought I already knew everything, and so there was no reason to question my own decisions.

At this time, I was running a company on the side called One of Ours Management, a music management company through which I managed two hip-hop artists. I got into this business because I always had a passion for music, especially hip-hop. So when I moved to Manhattan and began making money and regaining my confidence, I decided that I was going to go find an artist and try to enter that world. Around 2005, I started going to showcases around Manhattan. I finally found an artist that I really liked. He was raw, but he was winning some talent shows, and he wasn't signed with anyone. His stage name was Esso, but his real name was David Powell. I eventually signed a management agreement with him.

In 2007, I was at the height of my mortgage career, and Esso had reached the apex of his notoriety. He had appeared multiple times on MTV and was named "Unsigned Hype" by *The Source Magazine.*

We had a mixed tape that received rave reviews from all of the industry publications. At that time, we were having multiple conversations with record labels about signing him to a major record deal. The problem was that I was financing the business. I was spending about one-hundred thousand dollars a year investing in what I thought was going to be a big payoff in a record label.

Enter the financial crisis.

In both of my businesses, I had my expert blinders on: I thought I knew what I was doing, and I didn't pay attention to any warnings to the contrary. My mortgage business was growing, and now this new music venture looked like it was about to pay off. But then the financial crisis happened. Truthfully, there were a million signs that that crisis would hit the mortgage market. Wall Street had an insatiable appetite for mortgage-backed securities at the time because there was such a high payoff from them. Bankers wanted to offer more and more loans, and the only way they could do so was by lowering the credit score and down payment requirements, as well as by loosening income restrictions. At the time of the mortgage crash, we were allowing as low a credit score as 580, zero percent down payment, and no official documentation to prove one's income. Because I was in the business while this was becoming the norm, I didn't see it as a problem.

Meanwhile, there were people making millions of dollars shorting the mortgage market as the crisis happened! I didn't know enough to do the same. I think a lot of people *did* see the crash coming, but I was inexperienced and thought I knew everything. I thought I'd be great in business and great in music, but the world came crashing down.

Meanwhile, as Internet blogs got bigger and bigger, so did streaming. The record labels sued Napster, a competitor, and managed to shut it down. They thought they stopped the problem, but really all they did was delay the inevitable. By 2007–2008, streaming had become so dominant that the record labels decided not to sign any-body—they had no money to give. So now all of the deals that I had on the table went out the window.

I crashed in both the mortgage business and the music business. Because I had my expert blinders on, I didn't see either one coming.

Why Think Like a Beginner?

Thinking like a beginner allows us to create something that is new and exciting, and it makes engagement with ideas and projects fun. I maintain a beginner's mind-set by learning something new every day. I "read" daily for at least twenty minutes via audiobooks. The content is either entrepreneurial, about self-development, or business-related.

If we start our days by being open to learning something new, we will always be moving forward. This isn't as hard as it might seem. All it takes is an open mind and the decision to feed our brains wisely. Personally, I feed my brain by reading. In recent years, I've switched to audiobooks and podcasts in order to provide myself daily opportuni-ties to learn while multitasking. By listening to business strategies and inspirational stories, I've allowed my mind to acquire new skills. This can be accomplished by asking "why" when we hear ideas that pique our curiosity. Asking why and then allowing myself to think through the answers helps me to learn more and move forward from being a beginner to becoming an expert.

Thinking like a beginner applies to novel *adventures*, too. For me, starting a mortgage business was scary at first, but as I began to excel, I became more and more excited about the new job, which caused me to succeed even more. Eventually, I started to dislike the normalcy of my day, and I yearned for more. I had grown out of being a loan officer and wanted to challenge myself with something new. Six years later, while I was in my expert mind-set, the market had crashed. I was still clinging to my precrash status as a vice president of a publicly traded company, but that wasn't where I was anymore. Now, I was a broke *former* vice president in need of a job.

What ultimately saved me was going back to the beginning. I became a loan officer again, except this time, I had more knowledge, pain, and experience under my belt. I corrected the mistakes I'd made the first time around, and I became a bigger, better version of my previous self. Because of the darkness I felt following the crash, I found excitement in my new opportunity, and this was the beginning of my salvation. The experience helped me build a solid foundation for what would eventually lead to professional success.

When we think like an expert, we tend to let our egos get in our own way. But as children, we'll do anything, try anything, without hesitation or fear. As a child, we're always thinking like a beginner. We all remember what it was like to let our imaginations roam free. The most successful adults retain that youthful, ego-free imagination. They don't shackle their own potential with the arrogant, static mind-set of an "expert." The good news is that, no matter your age, you can always return to the beginner's mind-set. Don't let your potential suffocate under the weight of expert blinders. Instead, think like a beginner, and rediscover the fun of growing.

Takeaways

- It's not always obvious how a new, intimidating adventure can benefit other aspects of your life, but it usually will.
- When you wear expert blinders, you think you have everything figured out, and that you'll always continue to grow automatically. Expert blinders prevent you from adjusting to the world around you.

- *Don't* think like an expert, since it prevents you from taking in new ideas and keeps you rigid.
- *Do* think like a beginner, since this opens you up to new possibilities and keeps you flexible.
- Thinking like a humble beginner is an effective way to escape a growth trap.

Chapter Two—

Be Intentional about Growing

The Struggle of Comfort

By 2010, I was getting back on my feet following the crash of 2007–2008. I'd earned a spot as a mortgage executive once again. No longer selling loans, I was now helping to lead a startup that was growing rapidly. I had joined the company back in 2009 with a group of three other people with whom I'd worked in the recent past. The company was essentially a bank with all of the necessary licenses to sell loans, but it had no production. The two owners were sitting in a fully decorated office but couldn't make anything happen. The company was a shell of a bank when we joined as senior vice presidents of sales. At that point, we were high-producing loan officers and were looking for a bigger opportunity, so it was a good marriage. If everything went according to plan, we would all benefit financially.

About sixteen months after we cut a deal with the two founders, we had a sales floor in midtown Manhattan with fifty loan officers. I had assisted in setting up loan officers across Long Island, Phoenix,

Boca Raton, and Philadelphia, and we were working to expand into Charlotte. Everything was running just as I'd expected.

Thanks to this job, I had dug myself out of debt, regained some consistency and normalcy in my day-to-day life and was generally relieved to be back in a comfortable situation. There's that wolf-in-sheep's clothing of a word again—*comfort*. In hindsight, I realize that comfort is not a good place to be if you want to grow.

Because I'd gotten so comfortable, a few issues arose at the company that I didn't see coming. First, in building the sales team, we had far too many executives making big salaries, and not enough of us were doing the work to grow our production. We all were happy staying comfortable, and it showed in our overall effort. I myself stopped trying, stopped working as hard as I once had. Once again, I was expecting to grow automatically and failed to intentionally push myself to higher levels.

In January of 2011, the mortgage market took a brief downturn. That was enough for the owners of the company—who were still pretty inexperienced in their roles—to start tightening their ship by cutting some employees' salaries and firing others altogether. The first item on their agenda was to reduce the bloated executive staff salaries. Personally, I felt like I had done enough to prove myself worthy by traveling all over the country, being available whenever I was needed, and in general serving as a team player. But . . . I have to admit that I wasn't *leading*. I wasn't innovating, I wasn't growing. I was just existing. My salary was never cut and I wasn't fired, but the writing was on the wall for me. My fat and happy days at the startup were numbered.

Just going through the motions is never enough to grow, be great, or add value to those around you. A word of advice: if you ever feel the need to justify your job to people, then you're either in the wrong place or you're doing a bad job. If I'm being honest with myself, I was guilty of a little of both. Worse, I was using this as an excuse not to grow, and that resulted in my having no leverage in negotiating my salary with the heads of the startup.

The final nail in the coffin came when I heard one of my partners discussing with the CEO why he was a better fit than I was and that I needed to be let go. Afterward, my partner told me that he had told the CEO why I was great for the company. It was a naked lie. I had traded intentional growth for comfort, and finally I was paying the price for it. My life was upside down again, and my back was against the wall.

This Time, with Intention

To my credit, with no other options, I figured out my next move. A friend of a family member got me an interview with a small regional bank that was looking for a manager to start a new sales group. They wanted to grow, which, as you may have figured out by now, is an attitude that I'm always attracted to. I went to meet with them with nothing to lose. I put my best face on, and I nailed the interview. They called me the following day and asked me to come back to discuss joining their team. When I returned, I was told that I would be the head of a brand new consumer direct mortgage lending division. My position would come with a decent salary, an assistant, and a strong package of benefits that I'd receive once I grew the division.

"Hey, Ralph," the CEO said as we wrapped up our meeting, "I'm so excited for you to come in here and build this thing from zero to the moon."

"Wait, zero?" I asked, confused. "So I have no salespeople in this division?"

"Nope. Clean slate. You can do what you want."

I walked out of the office and called my fiancé, Beatriz—who would later become my wife—and told her what had happened. "The good news is, I finally have my own thing. No partners, no restrictions. I manage the business my own way and really grow it. The bad news is, we're getting married in six months, and I may not be making any money by then, since right now I have no employees to close loans."

To her credit, she believed that I could pull it off. Truthfully, so did I. I knew that all I needed was the opportunity, and here it was. I was determined to force growth by challenging myself. Unlike at the startup, I felt that I was in the right place for myself now. I was motivated and hungry to make this new venture work with intentional growth.

A year later, I had four offices open and two-hundred million dollars in closed loans, all under my direction. Unlike at the startup, I didn't allow myself to languish in static comfort this time. Instead, I went to work every day with the intention to solve problems and grow my division. This was the beginning of my growth as a leader.

Tom Brady's Drive to Grow

Tom Brady is arguably the most recognizable football player on earth and has been for many years. He might be the best quarterback of all time. No one would have predicted his glorious future when he started his college career at the University of Michigan. When he arrived, he was placed as the third string quarterback. Brady made no progress in his first few years at college: by his junior year, he was still third string.

Frustrated, Brady went into the coach's office and told him that he didn't see an opportunity for himself to grow. At that point, he started to feel depressed. He stopped trying, because he didn't have any hope that his career would turn around. Brady had given up on intention-ally growing, since he hadn't gotten ahead of the guys in front of him after years of putting in effort.

The coach told him that he was a good athlete, that he should know that he made the right choice with Michigan, and that he had to make it work. So Brady decided to stay. Unfortunately, he was given very little time on the practice field, which angered him yet again. How could he show the coaches that he was talented with such little exposure?

Brady went to a sports psychologist and told him about his issues. The man said to him that three reps were better than no reps, and that Brady should go out on the field every day and do the best he could. Brady couldn't control other people and their decisions, but he *could* control whether or not he grew as an athlete. And he did just that. Gradually, as he put intention behind his efforts, Brady earned additional daily reps. Eventually, he was moved into second string quarterback. From there, he continued to climb until he was starting quarterback for the rest of his college career. The rest is history.

Because Brady wasn't being recognized for the first couple years at the college level, he stopped trying to grow. As soon as he consciously tried to get better again, his career turned around. In the end, the only person holding Tom Brady back was Tom Brady.

Living Your Growth Plan

Once you're ready to grow intentionally, you need to ask yourself what your growth plan will be. If you don't have a plan for how you're going to progress, you will be swallowed up into someone else's plan. This happened to me at the startup I joined. Without our own plan, we'll inevitably be controlled by someone else.

Stop giving yourself excuses like, "I just need to wait until the time is right." At some point, we have to look in the mirror and decide to force growth with intention, full stop. At times, this will be painful, but we need to ignore the short-term pain and focus on our long-term goals in order to get to where we want to be.

Once you begin to implement your growth plan, don't be afraid to make adjustments along the way. In fact, mistakes are inevitable on the path to improvement. Most great leaders suffer many losses during their lifetimes. The key is to recognize when your growth plan is not working and to make changes before mistakes begin to compound. Replace ego with self-critical discipline, and you won't have any trouble modifying your growth plan.

Never compare your growth trajectory to those of other people. We are all unique in our skill sets and interests. Just because someone is improving and excelling according to their unique criteria doesn't mean that you can't do the same according to *your* unique criteria. Realize that other people will be more skillful and passionate in some areas than you are, but that goes both ways. The growth of other people has zero bearing on whether or not you succeed. Our only competition is ourselves. There are people who haven't even started their careers yet but will be more skilled than me in all sorts of ways. That doesn't mean I have to stop growing.

We have to get up and improve from who we were yesterday to who we want to be tomorrow. That's the only requirement for intentional growth.

Takeaways

- When you choose comfort over intentional growth, you fail to thrive.

- If you intentionally grow your leadership skills, you will likely succeed.
- Intentional growth is made much easier if you first develop a plan for yourself. Figure out which daily, incremental steps you need to execute in order to improve.
- Mistakes are inevitable, but how you react is not. Instead of giving up or letting frustration control you, make adjustments to your plan so that you can turn the ship around and continue to intentionally grow.
- The most fundamental requirement to growing intentionally is to get up every day and improve over who you were yesterday. Never allow yourself to "cruise" from one day to the next.

Chapter Three—

Recognizing Stagnation

Breaking Through and Rising Up

How can you tell whether or not you're in the comfort zone? And if you do find yourself stagnating, how can you break out of your funk?

Over and over, my life experiences showed me that being comfortable is never a good place to be. Whenever my growth has stopped, or whenever I stopped trying to become better, self-doubt and unhappiness start to creep in. I wouldn't say I get depressed, but I would say that stagnation sits very poorly in my stomach. Moreover, the negative mind-set that follows my stagnation always affects other aspects of my life, beyond where I felt stuck in the first place.

By 2017, I had become fully established as a recognized leader in the mortgage industry. I had been featured in *Forbes Magazine*, *The Wall Street Journal*, and *Yahoo! Finance*, as well as on Realtor.com and Zillow. None of these accolades helped me feel better about being in the same place, doing the same amount of business, not growing, and not trying to grow. By this time, my mortgage division was comfortably closing four-hundred million dollars per year, which enabled me to make a nice living, save money for my retirement, and give my family and my children things I never had. But I was not growing. The business I was doing was the same year after year: same volume, same people, same deals. My life was playing on repeat.

Between 2014 and 2017, I looked for other things to be passionate about because I was so dissatisfied with my job. During this time, I became a high-level endurance athlete, running Spartan Races and training seven days a week. I felt completely alive as I improved in my athletic abilities. Still, my "weekend warrior" activities weren't enough to make me happy Monday through Friday. I still wasn't trying to grow, innovate, or improve those around me. I would come into work and go through the motions for eight hours. I would pretend that I was the same person I had been when I began working in this division, but the truth was that I wasn't. I wasn't happy with where my career had taken me, even if my current position had once brought me fulfillment. My hobby of training for Spartan Races may have been a bandage, but the wound of my growth trap needed a more rigorous treatment.

A lot of us go through this stagnation phase every day. We show up for work, turn on our computer, browse through our phones, and look desperately forward to lunch and maybe an after-work activity. But generally, many of us are not enjoying what we do on a daily basis. When there is no joy, adversity, or improvement of your position, you're not going to be happy. No amount of happy hours, vacations, or hobbies on the weekend are going to make up for those eight hours a day you have to sit at your desk and/or look at your computer. That feeling of stagnation eventually affects other parts of your life: your physical appearance, your general well-being, and even your desire to become a better person will all suffer. We may not realize that remaining stuck and unhappy at our jobs damages the rest of our lives, too.

Toward the end of 2017, I had a wakeup call. I knew I had to grow my business—it had stagnated as much as I had. I had to be better than what I was, not only for myself but for all of those who were following me: both my family and those who worked under my leadership. After a couple of years of research, I made the decision to move my entire division to another company that I'd found. During my research, I had discovered that they were employing a novel, innovative technology called Octane. It was a proprietary software that I saw could revolutionize the mortgage business. More important for me, I appreciated its potential to take *my* business to the next level by making the customer and the employee experience better and faster. My decision was risky, since Octane was a brand-new software and had not really been tested in the market. After many meetings with those I trusted around me, as well as intense inner reflection, I decided that it was time for me to make the move. I had hoped that everyone would follow—and if they didn't, I would've made the move, anyway. It was time for a change.

During the final deliberations with my business partners, they told me that they believed in the move and in me. To my delight,

The top overall male City Challenger was Ralph Dibugnara. [Photo credit: Guj Koonar]

2015 Men's fitness Jersey City Challenge Race

even after what I had thought was a lack of leadership on my part over the previous few years because I was too comfortable and stagnant, everybody decided to follow me into the new venture. So, our entire division migrated over into a new system with a new software under a new business.

It was time to get uncomfortable again.

Moving a whole division to a new company was not going to be easy, especially with as many people as I had under my wing. Over the next twelve months, we made the transition. It was a challenge, but for the first time in years, I felt exhilarated. We spent millions of dollars that we didn't even know if we'd get back, but I believed in myself and in those around me. More important, I believed that, through this new venture, I could be a better leader, innovate more, and improve myself every day.

Three years later, I can tell you that I'm happy. Our business has grown from four-hundred million dollars to more than two billion dollars, and we are still growing. I took a huge risk, not only for myself, but for my entire team. But I couldn't continue heading down our path to nowhere, and I'm proud to say that I steered our division into a far more exciting and fruitful adventure.

Refusing to Stay Put in the Comfort of Riches

In the fall of 2008, Matthew McConaughey was already a huge movie star, but he had strayed away from his serious, dramatic roles and had became a known for his romantic comedy roles. For example, in the mid-1990s he had starred in serious films such as *Scorpion King, Lone Star*, and *A Time to Kill*. A few years later, though, he took on work in romantic comedies such as *The Wedding Planner* and *How to Lose a Guy in 10 Days*. He continued to be offered movie after movie, all in the romantic comedy genre. His stardom came with a huge salary and a comfortable life that he had grown to love. He had accepted being the "rom-com" guy. Eventually, though, he grew frustrated over not being challenged and found that he was unhappy with what his acting career had become. Because he was dissatisfied with how he was perceived by the industry—not as a serious actor, but as a romantic comedy star—he stopped striving toward his goal, which was to eventually win an Oscar.

He decided that he was done being comfortable and stagnant. McConaughey told himself that he'd no longer star in romantic comedies. He called his money manager and asked how long he could go without making any money while not hurting his family or his financial security. His money manager told him that he had saved enough money to be able to pursue his dreams, regardless of the risk.

McConaughey then called his agent and told him that he was done with rom-coms. He told him that he wanted only dramatic roles, and that he was willing to not work until that happened. McConaughey wanted to be challenged, and he didn't want to get stuck working on movies that he didn't truly love. The money didn't make a difference at that point.

Two years passed before the risk paid off. In the first year, he was still offered tons of rom-com deals. One even came with a price tag of fifteen million dollars. Impressively, McConaughey turned it down.

After his two-year, self-imposed exile, McConaughey had rebranded himself. Only by then did directors begin to look toward him as someone who could fill a dramatic role.

Finally, his patience bore fruit. First came *Lincoln Lawyer*, then *Magic Mike*, and finally *Dallas Buyers Club*, for which he would win an Oscar for Best Actor. He accomplished his dream. McConaughey's resilience and refusal to remain on his stagnant path resulted in earning the ultimate prize. His dramatic career has skyrocketed since then, and he has completely changed his image in the public eye.

While the story might not be relatable to everyone, since McConaughey is a larger-than-life movie star, what the actor has shown is that being comfortable and not being challenged to grow is something that even money, fame, and prestige cannot solve. If you're unhappy in your work, money is not going to make a difference.

Diagnosing Stagnation and Resolving to Change Course

How can you tell whether or not you're in a comfort zone and unhappy about it? For one thing, people in such a state will forget to value each customer, employee, or person in their network. They will take the people in their life for granted and treat them poorly as a result. I stopped placing value in my customers and my employees when I stopped valuing my job as a whole. Their experiences with me inevitably suffered. Another indication that you are miserable and stuck is if you feel unmotivated to improve yourself. When I felt like I was simply going through the motions with my company, I stopped regularly working on improving myself and the people around me through training, learning, and innovating. I stopped trying to be better at my job, and I stopped worrying about if my employees were improving, too. A third sign that you're dissatisfied is if you're not holding yourself accountable to standards of excellence. When you're unhappy, you don't care how you look or how you're perceived. For example, you might stop shaving regularly or dressing well. Also, you don't care *how* the work gets done, so long as it *does* get done. That attitude will never lend itself to making progress, either in your career or in your life more generally.

There are three actions to take to get out of being comfortable and extricate yourself from a growth trap:

1. Value your time. Ensure that you're getting the most out of the time you're working every day. It can help to establish a strict schedule for yourself.

2. Have a long-term plan of action. You will have to experience short-term pain to reach to your long-term goal, but that's the price you pay to climb out of the growth trap. Your long-term doesn't have to be five years out, or even six months out. Set out a challenging but realistic goal.

3. Work toward being better every single day and hold yourself accountable. Personally, I hire coaches, take courses, and make sure that I hold to a fitness regimen every single day. Without a means of holding yourself accountable, it's all too easy to slip into old stagnating patterns.

Takeaways

- If you have a dead-end job, feelings of stagnation and unhappiness eventually affect other parts of your life outside of work. In other words, misery in your career is not limited to the office, and you should take steps to resolve this.

- It isn't always easy to know if you're in an unhappy growth trap or not. Telltale signs include: treating others poorly, putting in minimal effort, and failing to hold yourself to standards of excellence.

- To get out of a stagnating comfort zone and growth trap, it can help to take your time more seriously, develop a long-term plan of action, and hold yourself accountable in your daily steps toward your long-term goal.

Chapter Four

Forcing Growth

A Career of Forcing Growth

At many points in my career, I had to make the decision to not waste time, take away all of my excuses, and place my back against the wall. As I have talked about in previous chapters, I was a bit stuck at the beginning of my career. I had to get past the mental block I had imposed on myself because I was unsuccessful at school. I had to get away from all the nonsense I had done in my adolescence that was still plaguing my psyche. I managed to take a step in the right direction when I took an all-commission job in sales. Gradually, I began to shake off my mental shackles and inch toward my goal of becoming successful in mortgages.

The financial crisis of 2007–2008 struck in the middle of my career. I lost everything: literally every single dollar I'd earned. And I was hundreds of thousands of dollars in debt to boot. But I didn't quit. Eventually, I returned to my roots of being a salesperson, I grew once again, I paid back all my debt, I regained financial stability, and, at last, I grew my mortgage company.

In recent years, I'd become too comfortable and financially secure, which served as an excuse for me not to force growth. Without any growth, I was unhappy. Eventually, I decided that enough was enough, and I dropped the excuses. As discussed in the previous chapter, I pounced on an opportunity to move my whole division to another company for better technology, more resources, and bigger opportunities.

In each period of my career, every time I took away the excuses, set a date to achieve a long-term goal, and put my back against the wall, it always worked out. Don't get me wrong—in every single one of these periods, I experienced failure, felt stress and anxiety, and went through moments when I didn't think I could do it anymore. But I always succeeded, because I refused to quit. I didn't let failure get in the way of my long-term goal. I put my back against the wall so that I didn't have a choice in the matter. I forced growth, and it ended in success.

Early in my career, I would only intentionally grow when I really had to, when the circumstances were dire. For instance, in between losing my job in 2008 and once again becoming a loan officer, I actually took two guaranteed salaries from companies that wanted me due to my past experience. In both cases, the companies closed before I had a chance to really thrive. But in all honesty, the guaranteed money would've just been a bandage to conceal my lack of consistency in personal growth. Nowadays, I recognize that growth must be forced even when I'm not in a desperate situation.

Learning to take away excuses and force growth will serve you in every single aspect in your life. You never know when the time will come, but if you've developed the ability to force growth, both you and the people in your life will reap the benefits in any situation.

Ralph and family

Growing through Dire Circumstances

In 2018, my wife and I went through something that forced us to put our backs against the wall and grow. There was a running joke in our family that I, a fitness fanatic who took literally thirty-six vitamins a day and never put anything in my body that I thought was unhealthy, somehow always came down with common colds. Meanwhile, Beatriz was never sick, even though she didn't exercise and ate whatever she wanted. She never even gained weight. It was almost like she had an ironclad immune system from birth.

Early in 2018, she started to feel sick for one of the first times in her life. First came stomach issues, followed by a rough cough. The cough kept getting worse and worse. She went to the doctor, who diagnosed her with multiple different ailments and prescribed her several antibiotics. But nothing seemed to relieve the illness.

I was convinced that she was walking around with undiagnosed pneumonia. Finally, frustrated with her doctor and the cumbersome process, I pleaded with her to get a chest X-ray.

Two weeks later, she received a call from the doctor, who said that she may have cancer. When I heard the news, it felt like a bad dream that I didn't think could possibly have been real. I believed that the doctor was wrong and so wanted to get another opinion from a specialist, especially because the original doctor thought that Beatriz's cancer was in her throat. She had never smoked cigarettes nor done anything else that would've caused throat cancer.

Through a friend, we were able to get an appointment that day with a throat specialist. The doctor looked at her X-rays and told us that he didn't think that the cancer was in her throat.

Something that Beatriz's original doctor had said stuck with me. She'd said that the cancer might've been in Beatriz's chest. And my wife's nagging cough kept ringing in my brain. I asked the second doctor if he'd looked at Beatriz's chest, and he told me that he wanted to do a PET scan. This is an imaging test that can reveal the metabolic or biochemical function of someone's organs. For our purposes, it can show where, if anywhere, there are diseases in a patient's body.

The doctor was able to pull some strings and bring us back the next day for the PET scan. I sat in the waiting room while Beatriz underwent the scan. I wanted to stand by Beatriz's side, but I couldn't. It felt like days, but in reality, it was only a few hours.

The doctor eventually gave us the bad news: Beatriz did have cancer, and he thought that it was Hodgkin's lymphoma. There are moments you never forget, and this was one of mine. Beatriz was hysterical, and I was numb. Over the next few weeks, we received calls from countless friends and family members with advice. They either had gone through a similar situation themselves or had known someone who had. When something like this happens, suddenly everyone comes out of the woodwork. Some offer their self-proclaimed expertise, others offer their own personal stories, and still others tell you what you should do. While I'm forever grateful for all of the love people offered us, it was a lot for us to take in at the time.

We started interviewing doctors who could treat her condition. After about a month, we chose Memorial Sloan Kettering Hospital. By this point, we were cornered like we'd never been before. At this time, our children, Lucas and Leina, were only four and two years old, and we had never faced anything like this before.

Ralph with family at children's birthday party
2 months after Beatriz's remission

This is an actual text message I sent to Beatriz after we decided on a treatment: "I want your treatment and recovery to be better than anyone else's has ever been. I want people not even to realize you're doing it, because it's going so well. I hate that everyone feels sorry for us. Everything is going to be perfectly fine. You'll be back to normal in a few months."

She responded: "It will be. We're going to overcome this. It's going to be tough, but in the end, it'll all be okay because we have a great foundation and we are both very strong."

But we couldn't have known just how tough that road would be. Again, when your back is against the wall and you're forced to grow through life, there are no guarantees. Regardless, whether the crisis is related to health, your personal life, or your own mind-set, you have no choice but to rise to the occasion.

Over the next four months—which was the time period we were told it would take for the chemotherapy treatment she was undergoing to be completed—Beatriz was amazing. She never even lost one string of hair. As we went through the treatment every week, she would come home exhausted, but to her credit, she'd appear strong and put on a brave face every day. If someone didn't tell you that she was sick, you'd never have known.

In March of 2019, we went back to the doctor after a final chemo treatment. We expected to receive the fantastic news that she was cancer-free. But then, as the doctor began to speak, I could tell immediately that something wasn't right. He told us that Beatriz had a form of lymphoma called "gray zone" lymphoma, which is a rare type of cancer in which the patient has both Hodgkin's and non-Hodgkin's lymphoma at the same time. From all of the disease spots that were in her chest, the doctor had discovered that one spot was still alive, which was now non-Hodgkin's lymphoma. So, the woman who had

had a perfect immune system her entire life suddenly possessed a dangerous threat inside of her.

The recommended treatment was more intense chemo. This time, Beatriz did lose her hair and a lot of weight. After the chemotherapy, she was to receive a stem cell transplant. Backed into a corner, what would we do now?

When we left the doctor's office, we had a similar conversation to the one we had at the start of this nightmare. We knew that we would do the best we could and that we would overcome this in a few months, totally in the clear.

This treatment was especially challenging. By the time we got to the end of chemo and began the stem cell transplant, I felt like we were in the homestretch. The stem cell transplant seemed like the easiest part of the process. I was wrong again. Beatriz had to stay in the hospital for five weeks for the transplant, which meant that I'd have to take care of the kids *and* make frequent visits to Beatriz and her mother at the hospital. Thankfully, we had plenty of help from her parents, my parents, and each of our siblings. But when it came to our children, I felt like it was *our* job to protect them and keep their lives as normal as possible throughout the process. We had hired a nanny to take them back and forth from school so that I could spend the day at the hospital and meet our children at our home after school.

I'll never forget Beatriz's first night at the hospital. I checked her into the hospital and left her with her mother, then I went to a work meeting in midtown Manhattan for the day. As I was walking back to the hospital from my meeting, my phone rang. It was the nanny, and she was uncontrollably sobbing.

"Ralph," she choked, "I was hit by a car crossing the street to pick up the kids. An ambulance is on the way, but nobody is going to pick up the kids."

"I hope you're okay," I responded. "Don't worry about anything. I got this."

I hung up the phone. I didn't even feel anything by that point. I had been trained by the last few months to not think and just follow my instincts. I jumped into a taxi, raced to the school, picked up the kids, dropped them off with my mom, and returned to the hospital. Problem averted.

Our nanny broke her leg, and it would take her months to recover. Fortunately, friends and family stepped in to help with the kids. Meanwhile, Beatriz continued down her road to recovery. We were all doing amazing things with our backs against the wall. We had no other choice but to forcibly forge ahead.

Beatriz pushed through and made it back to our family five weeks later. After another month passed, we returned for a checkup to make sure that the cancer was gone. We received the amazing news that she was officially clear of the cancer and that we were free to carry on with the rest of our lives.

At the time of this writing in 2021, Beatriz has been cancer-free for over two years. The stem cell transplant was miraculous. Memorial Sloan Kettering Hospital has even chosen her to be part of a commercial series that they are creating to highlight patients who have had success with their treatment.

The moral of the story for our family was that life tested us and forced our backs against the wall. We had to make sure that Beatriz survived, and we had to ensure that our children made it through as unscathed as possible. We accomplished both goals with flying colors because we took the attitude of, "Let's beat this, let's attack this. Let's not let this break up the family and scar us forever."

There were so many moments during my wife's illness when I felt utterly helpless and wanted to just sit on my hands and be told what to do by the medical experts. But my family couldn't afford such helplessness. We were even told by many that our marriage wouldn't survive the stress of the situation. Well, I refused to accept that. So, whenever I felt like I couldn't say or do anything to help, I put on a brave face and kept moving forward, even when I didn't know where I was heading.

Life will always throw you curveballs, and I've faced plenty. As I look back at them now, the only strategy that has ever worked was to force myself to face them head-on, to defeat the challenges, and to become a better person on the other side. I can honestly say that the darkest chapters of my life have been the best times, because they were always followed by success and personal growth. When I look back at the trying year when my wife was sick, Beatriz was an inspiration. She never questioned what she had to do. She just did it and never stopped. She didn't miss a treatment, she studied what was best for her, she did everything with a smile and never complained about it. When life gives you a challenge, or if you're too comfortable, I guarantee that if you take the attitude that you *must* grow, you will inevitably become a better person and a winner in the game of life.

Tips for Forcing Growth

How can you force growth?

1. Stop giving yourself excuses. "I'll start later." "I have plenty of time." "It seems too hard." These are all excuses. There *isn't* time. The answer is *always* to start now, because even when you do begin to grow, you will still have years to grow even further. There will always be more highs and lows before you master the craft that you are working on. Also, you have nothing to lose by starting. The worst case scenario is that you

fail, and even that isn't so bad. Failing is a lesson, and my best moments have come after my greatest failures. This is true not just for me, but for a vast number of successful people.

2. There is no such thing as a transition. Growth comes from putting your back against the wall and figuring out a plan to force growth. To me, transition has always meant doing something with half effort. No great result will come without your best effort toward your long-term goal. The longer the "transition phase" you grant yourself, the more you delay your best years of growth.

3. You need to manifest an intention to not quit and to suc-ceed by any means. Setting a long-term goal and/or putting a date on something has always been a great method for me to reach my goals. Leaving something merely *said* and not *set* by not putting a date or timeframe on it leaves you space for excuses. If I start a goal and tell myself I'm going to be great at something in three years, or if I have an upcoming event on March 6th, then I'm damn sure that I'm going to succeed by that date. Or, if I have one-hundred thousand dollars in credit card debt and I tell myself that I'm going to pay it off in three years, I now have a target that I'm forced to hit. This year, make your New Year's resolution concrete and quantifiable, rather than vague and general.

4. Time is the greatest obstacle to growing. The longer you wait to do something, the less likely it is that you will ever do it. Sometimes we feel like we have too much time. Everything feels like it can be done over years and years. The truth is you wake up and you're twenty-five, and then thirty, and then forty, and then fifty, and before you know it, you haven't done anything you'd set out to do. We have to do things

now. Time moves too fast. Minutes turn to hours, hours turn to days, days turn to months and years. Years in which you say that you're going to transition. Years that you tell yourself that you're going to do it next year. Years that you want this, but you can't do it right now. If you take away all of the excuses and put your back against the wall, I guarantee that you will reach all of your goals and aspirations in the long-term. There will be failure during that timeframe; there are going to be setbacks. There are going to be dark moments during which you think it can't be done. Stress and anxiety are natural feelings that we all have, but most of us don't realize that when we are stressed and anxious, we are actually growing. *Growth feels like stress.* It feels like pressure. It means we're moving forward. The greatest winners in the world fail, learn from their failure, and move on. There are no lessons in winning. Think about it. If we win quickly, what did we really learn? Most likely what happened was that we won because of the skills we were born with or because of knowledge that we already had. But if we lose, if we fail and quickly take a lesson from it and apply it to our long-term goal, the failure was time well-spent. So don't waste time—it's our greatest commodity.

Takeaways

- When you take away excuses, set a date to achieve a long-term goal, and put your back against the wall, you have a much greater chance of succeeding. To be sure, you will experience failure, experience stress and anxiety, and go through moments when you won't think you can do it anymore. But you can always succeed if you refuse to quit.

- In order to force growth, drop all excuses from your mindset, refuse to let setbacks discourage you, and never delay the start of your journey.

Chapter Five—

Pain as a Catalyst for Growth

P ain is the greatest catalyst for escaping the growth trap and fostering a growth mind-set. Early in life, pain was always something I avoided. I never wanted to be hurt or upset. But as I matured, I came to appreciate that my darkest and most painful moments were also my most empowering moments.

I hardly ever look back at my wins. Don't get me wrong—they're great. But I rarely draw inspiration from them. My losses and the times I was hurt, on the other hand, motivate me to try to never feel like I did in those moments ever again. I always accepted those failures, took lessons from them, and applied that newfound knowledge in the future. Thus, it was my losses, not my wins, that helped me better myself.

Crash and Burn, Pain and Learn

The 2007–2008 financial crisis hit every single pain point I could possibly imagine all at once. I should've seen it coming, but all of the pleasure I was experiencing prevented me from recognizing the pain that was on the horizon. There were plenty of signs that my life was about to explode. For one thing, my spending had gotten completely out of control. You don't have to have Ferraris and Bentleys to spend like there's no tomorrow. Unfortunately, anyone can spend without budgeting and/or living above their means, and I was certainly guilty of both.

Like most people in my industry, I believed that this ride would never end. I'd come to mortgages in 2001, and every year from then until 2007, I'd made more money than in the previous year.

During this time, I'd often go to Florida on weekends for business and then return to New York City for the week. One Monday morning in 2006, after I landed from Miami and took a cab to my NYC apartment, I immediately went to the ATM to grab cash to pay the cab driver. When I put my card in the machine, I was told that I had insufficient funds. I frowned: at this time, my gross income was higher than it had ever been. This should've been a pain moment, a learning lesson, but it wasn't. I was able to pull the money out of my overdraft account to pay for my cab.

I got into the hotel elevator, went to my penthouse apartment on the forty-seventh floor, and opened up my mail. In the envelopes were ten credit cards that offered cash advances based on my high income and the amount of debt the companies had seen me acquire. I took one of the credit cards, went online, and was approved for a $50,000 credit line. In my head, I had averted the crisis of running out of money.

I'll just make more money and pay this off, I thought to myself. *I'll use this new credit for now and keep this ride going.*

This reckless mind-set would come to bite me later on. I had accumulated about three-hundred thousand dollars of debt, on top of my mortgages. Including the mortgages, I was probably more than one million dollars in debt, but who was counting!

I'll never forget that day. I walked out of my apartment and headed to my office that was a block away from Wall Street. It looked to be a typical day—the sun was shining, it was beautiful out.

Boy, was I mistaken.

An email popped up on my phone that said that most of the mortgage products we'd been offering were soon going to be nonexistent.

This is impossible, I thought. *This can't be true. This is 90 percent of the business that drives my income. This has to be some kind of mistake.*

As I settled in my office and learned more about the situation, I realized that this was no mistake. In fact, the nightmare was just beginning.

I decided to end my day early and return to my apartment. As I watched the news, all of the banks were crumbling one by one. The unthinkable happened over the next few weeks and months. Bear Stearns. Lehman Brothers. Both were Wall Street stalwarts that had been around for years. They were staples of the industry, and now they were closing their doors.

As the next six months began to unravel, my company stopped doing mortgages, and I was forced to return to the job market. At first, it was not hard. I'd gotten an offer from a pretty large bank that was still in the business and wanted to move forward. I had to drive to Philadelphia for an aptitude test that they required of me as the final stage in the hiring process. I did very well, and they offered me a significant long-term guarantee to come onboard and grow my business once again. Crisis averted—or so I thought.

I should've known better. As I returned to my car, it started to rain. Soon, rain was replaced by hail. This was odd, since it was the middle of summer. Then, as I drove over the bridge, I heard a loud noise. My tire had just blown out. I got out of the car and started to change the tire. As I began, the jack slipped and slammed onto one of my hands. I managed to fix the jack, change the tire in one hand, drive home through the hailstorm, go to the emergency room to assess my fractured hand, and finally return to my New York City apartment. Sweaty, dirty, and with a broken hand, I dropped onto my couch. Despite the wild afternoon, I had just gotten a great new job, and I was happy to be moving forward.

A few weeks later, my euphoria came to a screeching halt. I saw in the *Financial Times* that my new company was about to close its doors. I opened up my email, and sure enough, that was indeed the case. I hadn't even started working there yet! Another pain moment.

I took this loss as a learning opportunity. I realized that I had mismanaged my money with frivolous spending and was not saving enough for turbulent times like this, and that I had to drastically change my relationship with money. Also, I had accepted the mentality that I'd be working for this company for the rest of my life, which was another mistake that I'll never make again. I had felt like I didn't need to know anyone outside of the company, and that I could work here for the next thirty years, like I'd seen my father and his peers do. They had held one job, stayed there, made a decent living, and moved on to a comfortable retirement.

In that moment of losing yet another job, I realized that your network is the most important thing you can have in your career. The people you know will always help you access things you wouldn't have been able to access otherwise. When my company closed, I knew nobody who could help me. The only people in my orbit were those who had also lost their jobs. We were all trying to find work for ourselves, and only the strongest would survive. No one was trying to help me, and I didn't have anyone who I could call.

It was time to get humble.

After a few months of wallowing in my pity and trying out some random lines of work—I spent a brief period a startup company with someone I'd worked with before, but that didn't pan out—I had to get back to reality. I was walking around with no money and no income, and I was foolishly holding onto my title as vice president of a publicly traded company. The problem was that nobody knew who I was, and I was no longer a vice president of anything. I was broke and out of work, a mortgage guy in an industry that was crumbling.

High school graduation

Finally, with my back against the wall, I decided to make a change. I moved out of my penthouse apartment and into a six-hundred-square-foot studio apartment back on Staten Island. I was too proud to ask for anyone for help, and I didn't want to move back in with my parents. I was just going to grit through this thing, because I didn't want to admit that I had failed and mismanaged my life.

Through a friend, I landed an interview with a mortgage company, Refinance.com, which was doing good things at the time and was still functioning in the business. That alone put it above most other mortgage companies. They had a loan officer position available. Part of me thought that I was too good for a sales position at this stage in my career.

I went to my interview with the CEO of the company, Jim Clooney, who would eventually become one of my business partners. My plan was to convince him that I shouldn't be just a loan officer, but rather one of his managers. He just needed to give me a shot. I put on my best suit and gave him the pitch of my life.

He looked at me in the eyes and said, "That's great, Ralph. But I have a ton of guys here who were vice presidents and managers at other companies. Right now, they're all selling loans and doing pretty well. That's the job I have for you. If you want to work here, you can. Hopefully, you will prove yourself and get to a managerial position in the future. But for now, working as a loan officer is ground zero for you."

I didn't have much of a choice, so I dove back into sales.

When I arrived for my first day with the new company, I walked onto a floor of about one hundred salesmen, and it was buzzing. I liked being around all of this energy again, but I was the low man on the totem pole. The sales floor was ruthless. People competed every day, and only the strong could survive. There was a limited amount of mortgage opportunities, which meant there were only a small number of leads being given out. The golden days were behind us, and only the best were going to really make a living at this now.

I still had hundreds of thousands of dollars of credit card debt, and I'd gone through all of my 401(k) money. I was pretty much broke, with no cash on hand. Out of stubborn pride, I didn't want to declare bankruptcy, give up any of my homes, or admit that I had failed. My only choice was to put my back against the wall, make as much money as possible, and dig myself out of this debt.

I wasn't at Refinance.com long before I met another one of my current business partners, Frank Capobianco. Frank was a young, dynamic sales guy, and he was number one at the company. I don't even think he acknowledged me for the first few weeks I was there.

After all, why would anyone acknowledge me? No one knew who I was. Still, he was who I needed to be if I wanted to achieve success as a loan officer.

I took my desk at the back of the room, and during my first week, I realized that everyone was working until eight or nine o'clock every night, plus weekends. Because I was the new guy, I wasn't even getting leads that the company was giving out. I was struggling to compete, even though I desperately wanted to.

At the beginning of my second week, I decided that I was going to change the game for myself. I was going to head to work when other people weren't there, which was difficult because they were working all day! I started showing up at seven in the morning, before anyone else would arrive. This way, the little leads that came early in the day would come to me. The problem was that I still had to work until eight or nine o'clock at night and on weekends.

These were long, dark days. I felt the pain, but lessons were being learned and I was digging out of debt. This would all serve to empower me in later moments of my life. Over the next year, I grew little by little, until I was in the front of the room getting the same leads as the top producers. I was making money again! With no choice but to make it my own way, I had learned to humble myself, persevere, and make something of my career once more.

This was the beginning of my new life in the mortgage business. My path was long and painful, but I took a lot of lessons from it. By the end of the year, I was back at an income level I'd been used to. I was paying off my debt, and I was competing with the best of the salesmen around me. I can't explain to you how much the pain from the previous two years of perseverance had made me a completely different animal, a completely different person. My new mind-set would serve me well for the rest of my life.

A few months later, Refinance.com ran into crisis, even though the leadership had been doing a good job. Over the next ninety days, they were set to close their doors as well. But this time, I was prepared. I wasn't going to make the same mistakes again, I wasn't in the same amount of debt, and I wasn't afraid of going back to selling loans. I was armed with the pain of the last few years, and because of that, the next transition was going to be a lot easier than the previous one.

My Father, the Noble Stoic

Pain and struggle don't have to be financial. They can be physical, emotional, or having to do with relationships.

Looking back on my life, my father was the biggest influence in shaping the person I am today. Interestingly, my father is a stoic man. He's not the type to tell you what to do or how to do it. He has always led by example. I believe that he developed his style of leadership through pain.

My father has been an educator for more than fifty years now, first as a teacher, then as a principal, and now, in his seventies, as a college professor and a program administrator.

He grew up in Brooklyn to an immigrant father, who had come to the country from Italy through Ellis Island at the age of seventeen, and to an Italian mother born to immigrant parents in Brooklyn. My father's childhood home held his two older sisters, a younger brother, and many aunts and uncles. It was a normal Brooklyn story for the 1940s and 1950s—a multigenerational home where everybody would come and go and where they'd congregate in times of need.

His father, Dominic, was also a stoic man who worked hard and did not believe in coddling or catering to his children. My father was told to get a job at the age of eleven, so he did just that, becoming a stock boy at a local liquor store.

My father's mother, Suzanne, was a sweet, gentle woman who cared for her children. She was their protector. She kept her children from their father's hardened ways and ensured that their lives were better each day than the day before.

There weren't any family vacations, except for the occasional trip to an uncle's lake house in upstate New York. There wasn't a lot of money to go around, so they made do with what they had, but that didn't leave much room for pleasure.

Sadly, Suzanne passed away at a young age. My father was only fifteen years old when she died of cancer. I believe that this was the first real pain in my father's life.

What happened over the next few years would change him—and possibly even me, down the road—for the rest of his life. His older sisters did not want to become the women of the house. Their father was rough and demanding, so they got married young in order to move out of the house by the age of eighteen. My father was left behind to fend for himself and his younger brother.

When my grandmother was alive, she pushed to put my very intelligent father in Catholic private schools. This cost money, but he flourished there. With his wife and daughters gone, my grandfather had no time to tend to my father's needs. Keep in mind, this is a man who came to Ellis Island at the age of seventeen by himself and was left on the streets of New York City. He didn't speak the language and had to make friends so he could survive. He wandered the streets until he found a friendly face that took him in and brought him to his family. It would be hard to expect this type of man to be soft on his son, despite the pain both must have been feeling over the loss of the house matriarch.

My grandfather had never even gone back to his home country to see his relatives after he came here. He was from a small town north of Rome called Bugnara. My last name, DiBugnara, stems from this.

With his mom gone, my father was told that there would be no more private school. Instead, he would go to the local public school and work even more to support the household.

My father was crushed. He felt like his choices were being destroyed. He decided that he would work even more than he had before to not only support the house, but also to make extra money to make his own way through private school. He would not ask his father for any money; he would do it on his own. Not only did he pay for school, but he had to take the bus for long hours through a not-so-great neighborhood. Alone in a rough neighborhood, he faced many trials and tribulations, fights on the bus, and long hours at work. Still, he possessed the determination to prove that he could do it on his own and go to college, which no one in the family had ever done.

My father would not only accomplish his goal, but he would surpass it and receive a doctorate. What he learned from the pain of losing his mother and having to fend for himself at such a young age was that he could make a better life for himself and his own family than the one he was offered as a child.

I have to tell you: my father has never, ever told me about his upbringing. He never told me these stories. I learned all of this second-hand, from other people. My father used his pain to lead his family by example—not only his two sons, but all of the students he taught and led throughout the years. My father's lifelong daily routine is now my routine, but he never told me to do it. Growing up, I'd see him wake up early in the morning to exercise, leave the house before five a.m., and sometimes not return until after eight p.m. He worked multiple jobs to give his family everything we needed. We were by no means rich, but I never knew it. I also grew up in a multifamily house in

Brooklyn, surrounded by relatives. He made sure to put me through Catholic private school throughout my youth and in high school.

Every summer, we'd get in the car and go on vacation. We even went to California when I was thirteen years old, which I'm sure took years of saving up. I have fond memories of my youth, and it shaped the man I am today. My father never told me I had to be great in school, or that I had to get a job as a kid. He led by example and let me make my own mistakes, find my own way—and he offered me a support system the whole way through. I had no idea that he was struggling financially or was stressed, because he shielded us from all of that.

My father showed us that there was nothing we couldn't do. There were certainly moments when I realized that things weren't that great, like when the door fell off of his old beat-up car while he was driving. I remember my father holding the door in one hand and driving us home with the other. But he never said that he needed more money or that we didn't have enough money. As a matter of fact, he made sure that I could do a bunch of chores around the house in return for an allowance, so that I could always buy whatever I wanted.

Like my father, I also got my first job around eleven or twelve years old, helping neighbors mow the lawn and rake leaves. My father never *told* me to do it, but I *wanted* to do it. Having seen the example he set, I wanted to be like him. I knew that with hard work, I could make money, and then I could buy things for myself and my family.

Both because he lost his mother at a young age and because he had to work hard for everything in life, he learned how to lead by example, and how to not make the same mistakes that his family made with him. My father's pain and struggle not only set him up for success, but they set *me* up for success without my even knowing it. It's only now, with the benefit of hindsight, that I can appreciate how my father turned his pain into a lifelong growth mind-set that, in turn, inspired me.

Pain will come in many forms. But if we use it for good, if we use it as a beacon of light to better our standing, we will not only help ourselves but all of those around us. The fastest way to grow is to apply what we've learned from our losses. We need to turn the hurt and pain into future wins and progress.

Here are five steps to help you grow from pain:

1. Look at each event as a test. Tragedy can strike anyone's life. I don't believe things happen *to* us, but rather *for* us. Painful events can be interpreted as life lessons that we can use moving forward. No matter what particular kind of pain we've suffered, we can learn from it by mining it for life lessons. Painful events and/or failure can be empowering, if we use them in the right way.

2. Success never comes easy. Always take a bad experience and turn it into a positive. The darkest times can be the greatest opportunities for growth. My darkest times in life were when I was the most broke, the most hurt, and the most emotionally starved. They have all served as empowering moments for me later in life. I turn to them every time I'm struggling or stressed. During these times, I tell myself, "If I made it through *that* painful experience of the past, I can make it through anything."

3. Life in our head is never quite the reality on the ground. We can only control how we respond to events. We tend to build things up in our head and make them seem weightier than they really are. We're usually our own worst enemy. But if we take those distorting thoughts, use our pain from the past,

and believe that we can push through hardship, we will always succeed. Our spirit and will are much stronger than we believe them to be. If we just take one step at a time, we will arrive at our destination. Don't make achieving your goals more difficult by making the journey look more challenging in your head than it really is.

4. You have to form new habits or strategies when bad things happen, or else they will happen again. If you don't learn from pain when trouble strikes and change your lifestyle for the future, then you are damned to repeat the same mistakes over and over again. The majority of successful people have undergone huge bouts of pain, changed their style and/or habits accordingly, and were better for it afterward. Later, when they faced the same types of problems, they met them head on and conquered them. It's our job to change how we do things to make sure that we are *better* from them, rather than *damaged* from them.

5. Take responsibility and embrace the pain. Blaming others will never help you make progress. Looking to others for blame isn't going to fix the problem or the pain or make us better. Instead, we can respond positively to our pain in order to ensure that we don't end up suffering from the same kind of pain down the road.

Takeaways

- It's not always helpful to look back at your wins. Losses, on the other hand, can motivate you to never feel like I did in those moments again. Accept your losses, take lessons from them, and apply that newfound knowledge in the future. It will be your losses, not your wins, that will help you better myself.

- You can learn from pain that is not only financial or professional.
- In order to learn from pain, look at each failure as a test. Always take a bad experience and turn it into a positive. You have to form new habits or strategies when bad things happen, or else they will happen again. If you don't learn from pain when trouble strikes and change your lifestyle for the future, then you are damned to repeat the same mistakes over and over again.

Chapter Six—

Get Comfortable Failing

Mistakes are a sign that we're actively working toward a win. This is one reason why it's okay to fail. In fact, it's actually your mission to fail. Times of failure are when you will learn all of the lessons that you'll need to eventually succeed. No one wins all of the time; no one reaches greatness by protecting themselves from losses. It is the losses that make you strong enough to do things you never thought you could.

In high school, I failed. In college, I failed. In the 2008 market crash, I failed. In becoming too comfortable, I failed. In staying fit, I failed. In controlling my emotions, I failed. And yet, none of these failures have stopped me from succeeding. I'll fail a lot more in the future, too. I'm far from perfect, but I'll never give up on being great.

In all my failures as a youth through high school and college, I quit after failing. In the early days of my career, I never learned to succeed because I kept quitting. If you do not enthusiastically try, then ironically, you cannot fail. If you don't fail, then you don't learn, and therefore you cannot possibly succeed down the road. Eventually, I learned that you want to fail as quickly as possible, learn from your mistakes, and then pivot accordingly.

I have been in real estate for twenty years now. My failures in growing my business as an entrepreneur are ingrained in me as much as my successes are. Every part of your career will offer opportunities to learn and grow following a failure. The most important lessons I learned from my failures came in three stages.

Too Inexperienced to Lead

Stage One: *I am my own boss now.* The most common mistake that young entrepreneurs make—and one that I have personally experienced—is becoming or wanting to become the person at the front of the room before you are ready.

For me, this happened when I was twenty-four years old. I was named vice president of a publicly traded mortgage company due to my sales performance and my work ethic. But I had no idea how to lead. Because I had no experience, when I stood in front of my new group of subordinates who were much older than I was, I assumed that they would respect me and follow my direction simply because of my title. I was very, very wrong.

Frankly, I had no substance, and more important, I had not earned their respect through the experience of battling alongside them. The first meeting I led was a complete disaster. During my first year as "boss," I lost my temper when I didn't understand office politics, which only deteriorated the little respect my subordinates had for me even further. I acted too much on instincts instead of seeking help from a mentor or personal research. When I failed my team, I didn't know how to pivot, so I would just keep heading down the wrong path.

But no incident from this period holds a candle to the first time I was asked to fire someone.

That day came when I was instructed by my superior to drive to our Long Island office to fire an underwriter who had been performing poorly and would not follow correct procedures. He was a man with twenty years of experience in the mortgage business and had come to us very highly recommended. I looked at it as an opportunity to prove myself to my superiors and to the company. But this meeting would be a deep dive into everything I was doing wrong as a manager.

End of my first year in mortgages, 2002.
My goal was to close a loan in every state, and I achieved it

When I arrived at the building and walked into this employee's office, I was nervous yet sure of my mission. In his office, the first thing I noticed was a pair of crutches. When I asked him what had happened, he told me that he had broken his right foot the night before and spent the night in the emergency room. His wife had had to drive him to work that day. Already, I knew that this was going to be awkward.

Still, I had no choice. I had to proceed with what I was sent to do. I asked him to hobble over to the conference room so that I could have a private conversation with him. I also needed a witness present for his termination, so I asked another manager to join us who was much older than me but who was supposed to be my peer.

That was mistake number one.

I'd find out later that this peer wasn't happy with my status, given my young age. Looking back, I suspect that he had very little respect for me at that point. I didn't recognize this at the time, because I had never encountered this kind of subtle hostility before. Only later did I realize that he wasn't an ally, but during this meeting, I was utterly naive. The lesson of choosing your allies wisely would serve me later in my career when choosing task partners.

I sat down and explained to the employee all of the reasons I had written down about why his performance was subpar. His willingness to change his tune when necessary was not what we had hoped for, and he would be terminated. I spoke fast due to nerves, and I figured he'd accept his fate and leave quietly. Quite the opposite!

Mistake number two: instead of having a conversation with him, I told him our issues with his performance in a scripted way, with no confidence and leaving a lot of room for interpretation and debate.

Over the next forty-five minutes, I witnessed a man go through every emotion. First shock, then sadness, and finally anger. As I sat by with no knowledge of how to stop this out-of-control freight train driving nowhere, the manager just sat there and watched me drown, never speaking or offering suggestions. This is someone who had been through this many times before, but he was going to watch me suffer.

Know your audience and your allies when making a plan. This is something that I learned that day and never forgot.

Without knowing how to stop this and with no help, I decided to let this uncomfortable chaos run its course. Eventually, he ran out of steam, told me to go screw myself, and hobbled out of the office. If all of that wasn't enough, I had to help him get a box, pack his belongings, and escort him out to the curb, where his wife picked him up.

That was an awkward fifteen minutes, but at least I learned important lessons about how to handle such situations in the future.

To reiterate, the biggest mistake I hear young entrepreneurs make is that they want to be their own boss. Wrong answer. To truly learn how to succeed, you need to learn from the mistakes of others who have already faced similar issues and fixed them. Learning from the failures of those who have come before you can be some of your most rewarding lessons. Working for someone else will give you perspective and knowledge of the past that doesn't cost you a cent, and you will experience processes without being responsible for them. It doesn't matter if the process that you're observing is right or wrong, you can learn from it either way. To be a true leader, you first need substantial experience. Ideally, this experience can be on someone else's time so that the inevitable mistakes won't cost you your livelihood.

When I was made a manager at such a young age, I came to appreciate the importance of learning from other people's mistakes the hard way—I ended up making my own mistakes instead! Still, I didn't let this kill me or make me want to quit managing. I went back to my office the day after I fired the underwriter, sat down with my manager, and explained to him what had happened. He then went through the steps that *he* would have taken in handling the situation, which made a lot of sense to me. Now, do I wish that he would have given me his wisdom beforehand? Yes. But then I never would have had that real experience that would serve me for the rest of my career. Find a mentor or leader who is willing to help you, use your time with them wisely, and then learn to pivot after receiving their advice.

Networks, Pivoting, and Remaining Confident

The next stage of my career can be summarized as, "I built it wrong and lost it all, now what?"

In my first days of success, I worked hard but not smart. I felt invincible, because I thought that the money would never stop coming and the business would never stop growing. I didn't anticipate the financial crisis of 2008. When that happened, it all came to a screeching halt.

How could I have avoided a catastrophe like that? As a boss, I felt like I didn't need guidance. What I needed to do were three things that I only learned from failing.

First of all, I needed to network more. The larger your network, the more options you will have at your best and worst times. Your network should be one to which you've provided value, so that when you're in need, those in the network know what your worth is. Eighty-five percent of business is done by word of mouth. Leveraging your network is one of the most important steps as you scale your business or your life.

Lesson number two: pivot fast. When the crash happened, I froze. *What do I do? Where do I go?* I thought to myself. When your business takes financial hits or when projects fail—and they will—the most important thing you can do is move forward, stay consistent, and find a quick solution. Standing still will never, ever get your business where it needs to be. As an entrepreneur, you will need to pivot fast and often. Failure is not a death sentence, it's fuel for business and personal growth.

Failure number three was my loss of confidence. Major failure will break you in ways you never thought possible. It will make you forget who you were before and what it felt like to be successful. All those thoughts of self-doubt are learning opportunities. We need to take those failures and examine what we did wrong and right, in order to ensure that the next failure will be far less disastrous. Success isn't a straight line. The best thing you can do after you are knocked off your track is to work your way back to success.

The Best Leaders Have Battle Scars

Stage three was learning to appreciate the difference between a field general and a tent general. You have to be able to do the job yourself before telling others how to do it. Early in my career, my problem was that I was trying to lead people whose jobs I had never done. I had become a tent general—someone who creates strategies, policies, and directions before doing any of the work themselves as a field general. A field general has battle scars and experience from all that they've already done. They have fallen, been battered and bruised, and learned from their mistakes. Only after all of this experience do they create strategies toward the same issues that a tent general might want to solve. Showing your team that you've been where they are is the best way to teach your followers how you've been able to complete the tasks that they are now responsible for.

Later on, as my career grew and I created large teams and companies, I learned from my mistakes and encouraged my teams to think on their own and solve their own problems. I gave my people adequate guidance so they wouldn't drown like I did when I received a lot of responsibility early in my career. I gave them enough information to know the pitfalls to watch out for, but I also gave them the room to think on their own and learn from their own experience. If you empower people to think intuitively, they will become masters of your methods and perhaps even improve on them. This is far preferable to them acting as robots that need your guidance on everything. If you are the only person solving issues, then your business or life cannot run without you. Be curious about your team's thoughts and opinions, as *they* can help *you* learn from failure and change.

Turning Failure into Innovation

Spencer Silver was a scientist at 3M from 1968 until 1996. One night, he was working in his lab trying to develop a very strong adhesive. Unfortunately, because of his inexperience, he suffered a misstep and accidentally developed a *weak* adhesive. Instead of hiding all of his mistakes, he decided to share both his process and his results with his colleagues so that they could collectively learn what he had done wrong. Following his blunder, Silver sought advice so that he could improve rather than hide his errors away or lie about them.

In 1974, Art Fry, a chemical engineer at 3M, heard about Silver's weak adhesive at a company seminar. Fry realized that this seemingly mistaken product was actually a solution to his problem. Art had been frustrated because his paper bookmark would always fall out of his book of hymns when he sang in church. The bookmark kept falling to the floor, and he would always lose his spot. Art realized that he could use Spencer's adhesive to make a bookmark that wouldn't damage his pages but would still hold the pages in place.

And so the Post-it note was created.

The Post-it note is considered one of the greatest inventions ever, with four thousand varieties now sold worldwide.

To me, what's important about the story is that more will come from *sharing* your failures and *working* on them than hiding them, because something great can always come from learning from our mistakes. We don't have to be world-renowned inventors to share our mistakes; we just have to be confident in our ability to *learn* from them and make progress.

Failing until You Don't

Denying the harmful effects of mistakes in your life can itself hamper your pursuits in many ways. Mel Robbins, who is now a legal analyst for CNN, was once a defense attorney and wrote the *New York Times* bestseller, *Stop Saying You're Fine*. It highlights her method known as the 5 Second Rule.

Mel discovered that denying that you're failing can become a debilitating habit. She first discovered this rule when she was out of work and broke. She had just lost her job with Fox, and her husband's business was failing. Her family was pushed to bankruptcy. Not only were they in a massive amount of debt, but she and her husband were on the brink of divorce, and she was drinking alcohol way too much.

Every night, Mel would make a plan to start over the next day. She would tell herself, "I'm going to get up, go to the gym, take a cold shower, feel better, come home, and make cold calls until I find someone willing to hire me." But every morning, she'd get up, open her eyes, and find herself not wanting to do any of those things. Rather, she wanted to stay in bed and let another day go by. In this way, Mel continued to be depressed and broke, and she wasn't doing anything for herself or her family.

One night while watching television, Mel saw a commercial about a rocket ship that was taking off. *Five, four, three, two, one . . . liftoff.* All of a sudden, it clicked, and Mel knew what she had to do. She decided that when she opened her eyes the next morning, she would only give herself five seconds to get up and begin to do what she told herself she'd do the night before. And it worked. This is how the 5 Second Rule was born: if you have an instinct to act on a goal, you must physically move toward the goal within five seconds, or else your brain will destroy your motivation.

She applied the rule the next day. Little by little, Mel's daily routine changed for the better. She began to exercise and make phone calls to try to find work every day, and she even developed more patience with her husband.

Eventually, she landed a job with CNN as a radio host. She also decided to share her 5 Second Rule with the world by writing a bestselling book about it.

Where Mel was failing herself was in her daily routine. I don't believe you have to have a five second rule to change your habits, but you do have to get past your feelings of dread and hesitation every day and do what's best for you. Admit that you're failing yourself, fight against your inner demons, and start moving forward. Look at your mistakes as opportunities for growth, not as setbacks. Use them to create new habits and move forward. Mel used the lessons she learned in overcoming her self-imposed barriers to become a bestselling author and renowned television and radio host. Once you fix your daily routines, what dreams will you accomplish?

Takeaways

- No one reaches greatness by protecting themselves from losses. It is the losses that make you strong enough to do things you never thought you could, because you can apply the lessons learned from failure toward future successes.

- The most common mistake that young entrepreneurs make is becoming or wanting to become the person at the front of the room before they are ready. It's perfectly fine to work for someone else for a while and learn from them before venturing out on your own.

- When your business takes financial hits or when projects fail—and they will—the most important thing you can do is move forward, stay consistent, and find a quick solution. Standing still will never, ever get your business where it needs to be. As an entrepreneur, you will need to pivot fast and often. Failure is not a death sentence; it's fuel for business and personal growth.

- Be very judicious when choosing whom to collaborate with. Make sure that your colleagues have your best interest in mind and that they won't stab you in the back for their own selfish purposes.

- Be a field general, not a tent general. A field general has battle scars and experience from all they've already done. While a field general has shown his/her team that he/she is capable of doing the job, a tent general has never left the ivory tower. Showing your team that you've been where they are is the best way to teach your followers why you are successful.

- The invention of the Post-it and Mel Robbins' 5 Second Rule teach us that failures are not always destined to be permanent. The Post-it was born out of what was thought to be a creative failure, and Mel Robbins took her daily five seconds of indecision and turned them into a motivational springboard. Whatever your current failures are, think of creative ways to turn them into tomorrow's successes.

Chapter Seven—

Forming Habits after Failure

Failure is only a permanent loss if we quit. Indeed, failures can be our greatest learning experiences. So, unless we decide to stop moving forward with what we are doing altogether because of some minor failure, then we have an opportunity to gain more than we've lost following a setback. The difference between winning and losing, or between succeeding and failing, is habits. In hindsight, all of my failures have caused me to form new habits.

Failing on the Court

When I was younger, I had a lot of bad habits, and I rarely changed them after failures. A prime example is my childhood basketball career. Every year, my junior high school would have something called sports night. They would put one team of kids against another in three different sporting events. *My* event was basketball. At the time, I was the best basketball player in my class, the M.V.P. of the school, and the best in the school league. I was eager to play on sports night to show my family and friends just how good I was. I planned to dominate the game and earn my class a win. Before the game, people even said that if I would get us a basketball win, then we'd be very likely to win the entire sports night. Everything rested on my shoulders.

When the night came, the gym was packed, my whole family was there, and I was excited. I was really confident going into the game, but our opponents double- and triple-teamed me all night. Every time I touched the ball, multiple players from the other team piled on me. After just a few minutes, I knew that this was not going to be a good night. I don't remember much about the game except that we lost. I played terribly, didn't score much, and let my class down because of my inability to handle the pressure of being attacked my several opponents at once. I didn't have the mental agility to pivot and change my plan to adjust.

I was so fragile that I quit basketball entirely after that night. At twelve years old, I left the court feeling completely defeated. Later on, I was talked back into playing again, but I was much less confident than I used to be. I was afraid that if a challenge like the one I faced on sports night rose again, I would fail. I didn't know how to develop new habits to prevent a double- or triple-team approach from defeating me a second time. All I could do was hope that it would never happen again.

I had a *reactive* mind-set, rather than a *proactive* one. A proactive mind-set considers ways by which you should prepare yourself for the failures that will inevitably arise and the steps you could take to change your path accordingly. A reactive mind-set is a state of mind in which you passively wait for unexpected problems to strike and refuse to think of creative solutions. A person with a reactive mind-set is likely to face the same failures over and over since he/she never adjusts their actions after a failure.

The year after I lost my confidence on the basketball court, my family moved from Brooklyn to Staten Island. I had to start completely over with a new basketball team. I didn't know any of the players, and I had to prove myself all over again. As a shy kid entering a group in which everyone already knew each other, it was an uncomfortable atmosphere for my reactive mind-set. I made the team, but as the season went on, I didn't make it off the bench once. I made it through the year contributing basically nothing. My confidence was broken even further, and I wanted to quit all over again.

Still, I wanted to make the team the next year, mostly because it was what I thought I was supposed to do, even if it wasn't something I really wanted to do. I didn't change any of my habits, so I was stagnant. I had no real confidence that I could make the team. Freshman tryouts came and went, and I didn't do well. My previous failures on the court were still messing with my head. In the final cut, the coaches dropped me. Instead of forming new habits so that I could improve my game, I quit trying at basketball for the rest of my time in high school. I still played in some other leagues, but I never even attempted to play for my high school team again.

The mind-set of quitting when things got hard was a detriment to me all throughout high school and college. It affected my grades, my social life, and the other sports I participated in. I'd quit anything that started to feel difficult. Because I had the mind-set of failing and not fostering new habits and then trying again, I kept failing over and over and not improving.

My Daily Habits

I had a big failure in 2008. After I had enjoyed many successes in my career and finally built up my confidence, quitting was not an option. This wasn't because I had suddenly become more enlightened, but rather because my back was up against the wall. I had bills and people depending on me, and I had to work to meet all of my responsibilities. With no option to quit, I formed new habits that would serve me for the rest of my life.

Why is it sometimes helpful to be cornered by life in order to form new habits? If making my high school basketball team was a do-or-die scenario, I guarantee that I would've figured out how to make it. This tells us that changing our habits is ultimately a mind-set issue. Mentally, if we stop giving ourselves the option of quitting or not changing our habits, then we give ourselves an opportunity to grow.

My habits have been pivotal to my growth. These are my current daily habits that I have improved on and sharpened over the years.

1. I stick to a daily exercise routine. Whether it is exercise or something else that brings you joy, find an activity that's healthy for you and for your long-term physical and mental wellness. Practice it daily or almost daily.

2. I spend a portion of every day networking. It isn't always traditional networking, but I stay in touch with old associates and friends, *and* I strive to meet new people. I keep the communication genuine. This can be through social media, text, email, phone, or video calls. Be proactive in meeting new people, since it helps all parties to grow.

3. I try to expand my knowledge every day. Reading or listening to positive stimulants, studying my market, and expanding and improving an aspect of my business or life are parts of my daily routine. The more we consciously consume positive and fruitful information, the easier our growth will be.

4. I incrementally complete short-term goals that help me build toward my long-term goals. A long-term goal does not have to be five years in the future. Make a six-month plan that allows you to change direction when needed. Nothing should be so completely set in stone that you can't go back to the drawing board if necessary. You are going to improve by failing, not by

making a perfect plan that never gets off the ground because you're too afraid to start. I work on small, day-to-day wins and losses. When I fail on this small scale, I adjust my plans. A stepwise process will help you grow toward your long-term goal, since it compounds over weeks, months, and years.

5. I find a way to meditate or relax my brain in a manner that is healthy for me. Find something you can do every day that relaxes you but does not harm your wellbeing (not drugs or alcohol). A good rule of thumb is that an activity that does not require you to consume anything is more likely to be healthy than one that does require physical consumption.

6. I delegate. Find people around you to whom you can hand over responsibilities. This way, you are able to operate productively and efficiently with the tasks left in your lap. Delegation also allows you to concentrate on your long-term goals and move toward them. Furthermore, you need activation partners around you. Sometimes you'll have a great idea but not the right people around you to put them into practice. Having people to whom you can delegate tasks frees you up to engage in other pursuits that you're more suited to take on.

7. I manage my time as if someone is paying for it. In practice, this means that I aim to fill my time in meaningful ways. Wasting time is the worst thing people who aspire to success can do. To spend my time wisely, I schedule meetings and time blocks. President Obama used to schedule his entire day in three- to five-minute intervals. This isn't uncommon for successful people. Even if you're not yet busy or succeeding, it's still important to manage your time. Organize your day by making sure it's filled with things that benefit you mentally and physically. This is possibly the most important habit to foster.

8. I fail fast. I've learned how to recognize when something isn't working and change course immediately. Every day, I try to learn from my mistakes and improve moving forward. To do this, you have to develop a habit of recognizing mistakes, acknowledging what went wrong, and coming up with a solution that works for you and will prevent the problem from reemerging in the future.

9. I always have my eye on a long-term, primary goal. In my life, a million things are always going on at once. No matter how chaotic your life is, never lose sight of your most precious goals. Don't lose focus on your primary mission, and don't get distracted by short-term losses or unexpected setbacks that stall your growth.

10. The one-touch rule: answer emails and text messages when they are received. Don't read them and then save them for later. If you do, you will have to reread them, which is a waste of time. Instead, read them, answer them, and move on. This can also be done in a way that conforms to your schedule: do not look at any emails or text messages unless it's during your scheduled time to do so. So, book time throughout the day during which you plan to read your messages, and be regimented about ignoring incoming messages until the scheduled time comes.

Because of my failures in 2008, I learned that having a routine and effective habits can get you through anything, and that no failure is ever a permanent setback unless we let it beat or kill us. My biggest failure created my best mind-set. In the years since 2008, my routine has still evolved, but I've always *had* a routine. Once I was faced with a massive failure and was forced to climb out of it, I developed new habits that have helped me to this day. My habits keep me focused on what I have to do for the day. This erases some of the anxiety, stress, and pressure that we all face in our daily lives. Most important, my routines create a predictable structure for my life: I get up in the morning knowing that some of my tasks are exactly the same every day. This consistency alone takes a lot of life's pressures off the table. *That* is the beauty of habits.

Let me give you an example. My routine between 4:30 a.m. and 9:00 a.m. is the same Monday through Friday. I get up, clear my mind through either meditation or just sitting in the dark, and take a cold shower to wake my body and my central nervous system up. Then I start my exercise routine, which lasts between sixty and ninety minutes. While I exercise, I listen to either an audiobook or a podcast. Audiobooks are a part of my life seven days a week. I have a timer set on my phone so that I am forced to listen for at least thirty minutes every day. For me, audiobooks are a source of inspiration for how I can grow as a person. Sometimes I read books that are entertaining but still inspirational, such as an autobiography about someone who overcame a life that they thought they could never escape to eventually succeed beyond their wildest dreams. The process of feeding my brain while exercising gives me the energy and motivation I need to start and succeed in my day.

After my early morning routine, I head to the office or wherever I need to be in order to start working. My initial work routine begins

Ralph on FIOS News 2016

Ralph on CBS News 2015. First tv broadcast appearance

with my to-do list that I create the previous night. These are tasks that I absolutely need to complete that day. My to-do list helps keep me organized around what *has* to be done and what *does not* have to be done that day. As important as your to-do list is for the day, your "not" to-do list is just as important. In addition to tasks that can wait, on my "not" to-do list are things that will distract me or knock me off my goals. I leave reminders for myself not to focus on those things for the day. They say things like, "Do not get distracted by social media." "Do not stray from your routine." "Leave time for yourself every day to be creative, and to clear your mind." "Don't fill your brain with unexpected stress or distractions."

I try to take care of all of the tasks on my to-do list between 7:30 and 9:00 in the morning, before all the rest of the distractions bombard me and I lose control of the day. Next, I clear up my email inbox and respond to any text messages that require my attention. That means deleting any emails that are unnecessary or that I already took care of and moving other emails into folders that I set up to keep myself organized such as "bills that need to be paid," "important documents," and "tasks to do."

Once I finish my to-do list and clear my inbox and text messages, I am ready for the day. Sometimes, by finishing all of my urgent tasks, new problems emerge, and so I end up with yet another to-do list. By this point, I usually delegate tasks to my employees in order to juggle all of my responsibilities. I also review my calendar and my timeframe for all of the other things I should complete within the next six to eight hours of my workday.

By having a schedule, a to-do list, and a routine in the early morning, I am able to control my day. My daily routine between 4:30 a.m. and 9:00 a.m. anchors me in an almost spiritual way. After the official workday starts at 9:00 a.m., when things happen that are beyond my control or that I couldn't anticipate, or when I am pulled in a million directions, I have a calendar to keep all of the chaos in order. During the challenges of the day, I am focused and stable because of my morning routine. It provides a solid foundation that lets me handle all of the unpredictable stress that life throws my way later in the day. My routine and scheduling allow me to go into tasks without stress. Even more important, because I'm so diligently scheduled, if I finish things early or if something gets canceled, I suddenly have time to do things I like to do, be creative, or spend more time with my family.

The four foundational principles of habit formation are:

1. **Long-term focus is the ultimate foundation of habit formation.** We all go through short-term pain to reach our long-term goal. The key is to create your long-term goal with a focus on incremental growth *toward* that goal. Remember the importance of incremental progress as you go about your daily activities. My daily routine includes reading, fitness, and educating myself. I know that doing just a little of all three every

day makes me better in the long term. Sure, you might suffer short-term slips and failures, but those are just small setbacks to your long-term success. Strong, consistent habits will enable you to put money in the bank every single day with respect to your personal growth. That "money" compounds over time, and your everyday short-term growth will add up until you reach your long-term goal. Long-term thinking also allows for self-innovation. When you're making changes in your life routines and growth patterns, you're inevitably going to have failures. If you have a long-term goal, then short-term failures won't discourage you, and you'll be able to use the failures as a springboard to innovate into a better version of yourself.

2. **Add the right accountability partners to your circle.** To create good habits and routines, you might need some help. For me, it's not always easy to do well in my health aspirations. For example, I want to eat right every day, but I am always tempted by sweets, sugar, and other junk food. So I hired a nutritionist who makes me check in once a week with my weight goal and eating routine. I even send him photos of myself. Every Friday, one way or the other, I have to show up and tell him what I did. It keeps me accountable, and so I don't stray too far from my diet and gain weight. Whatever your goal is, you can find a way to keep yourself accountable through other people. The examples span the range of potential human endeavors: a gym partner to motivate you to work out, a book club to force you to read, or a networking group that meets once a week to discuss how to earn more money. Find people who will keep you accountable to your long-term goals, which could be better finances, better health, or a better social life. It can help to find people who have the same goals as you so that

you help each other in a mutually beneficial relationship.

3. **It's not about whatever everybody else is doing.** In a world of social media and constant comparisons, we look at our peers and judge them over how well or badly they're doing. The simple truth is that you just need to concentrate on how *you're* doing. I can compare this to an idea of Amazon's. One of the company's core principles is to focus on their *customers* and not on their *competition*. The company has been successful year after year because they focus on improving their own processes and satisfying their customers rather than on what their competition is doing. For example, by allowing customers to buy goods using pre-set options, rather than having to tediously insert their credit card and shipping address every time, Amazon gives their clients an extremely user-friendly experience.

4. **We need to do better for ourselves and not for anyone else.** In any case, what you think is a reality on social media is most likely not a reflection of the truth. Most people are not going to show you the low points of their lives online; they are only going to show you their highlight reel. As people who are trying to develop good habits for long-term growth, we need to focus on us and only us. We are our greatest detriment when we feel compelled to keep up with other people. Trust me, no one wins all the time, no one's life is as good as it looks on social media, and on top of that, it doesn't matter. All that matters is what we are doing to better ourselves.

5. **Surround yourself with the right energy.** Outside of accountability partners, we need positive people and influences around us. This applies to our daily routines as much as to any other part of our lives. Personally, I don't watch the news, I don't read the papers, and I try not to watch too much television that would put

negative energy in my brain. We don't realize that what we hear and see every day can influence our overall attitude and habits. If I watch a sad television show or a video that does not motivate me to do something that brings me closer to my long-term goal, then I'm just hurting myself. Every day, I am conscious of what I am feeding my brain. Ask yourself: what are you doing on a daily basis that makes you not want to grow? For example, you could be spending too much time with a family member or friend who always complains or discourages you. Your growth has no time for those kinds of influences. Find people that make you want to be better, get up, do more, and innovate. Surround yourself with influencers who motivate you toward your long-term goals and encourage you to establish better habits.

Takeaways

- It is important to develop a proactive mind-set—one that allows for novel habits to form in the face of unexpected setbacks so that you will be ready the next time you face a problem.
- Daily habits keep you focused on what you have to do for the day.
- Manage your time as if someone is paying for it. Wasting time is the worst thing people who aspire to success can do. To spend my time wisely, schedule meetings and time blocks. Organize your day by making sure it's filled with things that benefit you mentally and physically. This is possibly the most important habit to foster.
- The four foundational principles of habit formation are: 1) focus on the long term, 2) find accountability partners, 3) don't worry about what others are doing, and 4) surround yourself with the right energy.

Chapter Eight—

Pivoting When Stuck

N o amount of studying is going to make us as smart as Einstein. No amount of practicing our jump shot is going to make us as good a basketball player as LeBron James. However, we *can* study or work hard at anything and develop a surprising amount of skill in that domain. We can become adept enough to compete with the best in most fields by sheer hard work, even if we are not born with inherent skill or passion. We have the power to maximize our capabilities and transcend self-imposed limits. But we have to *choose* to put in the required effort in order to do so.

If you're figuring out how to grow, ask yourself: are you working hard but on the wrong path? Sometimes, we are going one hundred miles an hour for a long period of time toward something we may not even want, whether it's financial, personal, or emotional. Many of us have patted ourselves on the back for working hard at our job, our business, our personal goals, or our relationships with other people. However, keeping your nose to the grindstone is wasted energy if you're working toward something that will ultimately make you miserable. An underappreciated key to growth is knowing when to change your path when you realize that it's the wrong one for you.

One kind of growth trap is getting stuck in a rut of daily efforts that, while they may be effective, are taking us down the wrong path. To honestly analyze whether or not we are on the right path, we need to ask ourselves a few questions.

The first question to ask is: what am I naturally great at doing? Most of us will reach for something easy and give an answer like, "I am a fast runner" or "I'm great at math because I can add in my head." Those answers are too superficial. We need to dig deeper to discover where our true talents, passions, and potential lie.

My Brother, Master of Psychology

In addition to having a huge personality, a lively and creative mind, and an ability to laugh at practical jokes before anyone else picks up on them, my older brother Michael is also a charismatic force of nature. Despite these impressive traits, the skill that makes him elite at what he does is his ability to use empathy. Empathy is the ability to share and understand the feelings of another. Like me, Mike wasn't a great student, and in retrospect, it was probably because he wasn't being challenged the right way. Someone like Mike, whose skills rest in understanding others, needs to be constantly interacting with people, or else he becomes complacent and occasionally disruptive. Mike was always in trouble in school for talking too much and making jokes. Every year in elementary school, I would start a new grade only for the teacher to tell me, "We're not going to put up with any misbehavior from you. I know how your brother acted. If you act at all like that, I'm going to throw you out." Mike would give the teachers psychological angst because he needed the interaction. If he wasn't going to get it in a constructive way, then he would get it however he had to, regardless of the consequences.

When he graduated from high school and went on to college, Mike decided to study psychology. He's never told me that he chose psychology because he was fascinated with how other people thought, but to me, it was more evidence that he loved to empathize with others.

Once he graduated from college and decided that pursuing a doctorate was not for him, he ended up in sales, like me. He worked in the printing and marketing industry because there were no other jobs at the time, and that's what he was offered. At first, this was perfect for him, and he excelled. He was great at speaking to people, understanding what they needed, and finding ways to either get them what they wanted or persuade them they needed what he was selling.

Because of his success as a salesman, as well as his ferocious independent streak, he eventually gravitated toward owning his own small company in the industry, with a partner who was doing something similar in the same business. Unfortunately, this is when Mike's growth trap began. Sure, he was making more money, the business was growing, and everything seemed great for a while. A growth trap can fool you into thinking you are on the right path, even when it feels wrong. There will be tension, because society or the people in your life will deem you successful, even though you might be miserable.

As business grew over years, Mike was forced to become an executive. This came with constant money conversations—tedious meetings about budget and bonus compensation for his partner and employees—and the responsibility to fire employees and make tough decisions that were less about how someone else felt and more about numbers. This was all difficult for Mike. Years would go by like this, and when he and I talked about it, I could hear how unhappy he was.

Like most of us do when we are stuck in the rut of a growth trap, Mike would look forward to vacations, nights out, and adventures. He wasn't growing anymore, because he stopped doing what he was so great at.

When we were growing up, he was the person I looked up to, because he could walk into any room and talk his way through anything. Mike could also turn any moment into a light one and get us access anywhere by using his empathetic skills—understanding what the person was looking for, asking for, or restricting us from. He could understand what moves a person better than anyone. It came so easy to him.

When a disabled friend of ours wanted to come to our beach house and stay overnight, it was my brother who had no qualms about bathing him, feeding him, and introducing him to girls in the crowded bars of the Jersey Shore. Mike knew that our friend needed to feel normal again.

Mike called me one day to tell me he was thinking of walking away from his business and starting a creative agency with his wife, Keily. His main functions would be selling, speaking to his clients, and curating the talent that he would be hiring. I said to him, "Hell yes." I knew he'd be going back to what he was best at. He'd be happy, good at it, and if he put the work in, maybe he'd even excel.

From the outside looking in, Mike had been making good money at his old job and providing a wonderful life for his family, so why would he quit? That's what a growth trap does to us—it sticks us in some place and tells us to stay there, stop growing, and ignore what we are great at.

Keily is great at being a manager and making sure that every detail is covered in order for a trip, project, or business to run smoothly. She is extremely forthright, sees black and white, and is all about the facts.

Keily is a perfect business partner for someone like Mike, who needs interactions with others in order to thrive. With Keily running the operations, Mike doesn't have to be stuck in the everyday functions of his business, which was what made him miserable at his previous job.

Finally, Mike was able to point his skills of empathy at the right projects by digging deep and thinking creatively about how to climb out of his growth trap. I'm happy to say that Mike and Keily's creative agency, Likey, has been greatly successful in its short three-year history, and its future is looking very bright. They have huge corporate clients like Sabra, Weight Watchers, and several talent agencies. This all grew out of Mike's choice to break out of his trap and follow his greatness.

Me, Michael DiBugnara, and Ralph DiBugnara Sr., 2020

Living in the Present

The second question (which is really three related questions) you need to ask yourself is, "Am I operating my life in the present? Or am I stuck in the past? Or am I imagining how great things will be in the future without doing anything to reach that dream?" When we use our past experience to solve problems in our present, we are progressing and avoiding the growth trap. When we feel the need to talk about our past accomplishments because they are more impressive than what we are doing today, we are holding onto something that is inhibiting our ability to make progress. It's great that you were prom queen or valedictorian, but how is that helping you today? If you were a star athlete in high school, that's amazing, but what skills are you using from that to benefit yourself in the present? If you landed a high-paying job right after college, good for you, but how has your professional trajectory been going since then? If you are clinging to how your life used to be great rather than accepting the state of your life now, then you are holding yourself back and getting caught in a growth trap. When we focus on the present day and live every moment like we can improve—because we can *always* improve—we will continue to progress and avoid the growth trap.

Obsessing about the future can also be debilitating as a mental process. If your mental process includes thoughts like "I will get to it" or "I will do it tomorrow" with no action plan, you will continue to disappoint yourself over and over. Comfort and fear will keep us stuck in whatever we are currently doing forever, unless we turn desire for change into action. I know it can be scary to go out and do what's necessary to change, but you must accept that progress is rarely easy to achieve. Some people are stuck in a job, relationship, or mind-set because of the sheer fear of what's next—the future. Predictions of the future without a plan of action can be our greatest copout and the largest reason why we remain stuck.

Running with Brutal Honesty

The third question to ask yourself is, "Are you being brutally honest with yourself?" This is sometimes hard, but it is the greatest way to remove insecurities. Honesty will light the fire in your belly in order to overcome your insecurities. For example, if you are out of shape, then tell yourself that: "Hey, you're being lazy, and you need to get help."

For me, being honest with myself has always helped me to improve my choices later on. Between 2014 and 2018, I competed in Spartan Races at the competitive level, running each race for prizes. These races were scored on a point structure, and runners were ranked at the end of the season. Spartan Races are between three, ten, and fifteen miles and include physical obstacles you have to overcome.

In the majority of those years, I ranked between the top one hundred and top twenty runners in the entire country. For someone who had previously never run around the block in my life, this was a pretty amazing accomplishment for me.

I also learned valuable lessons about being honest with myself.

In February of 2015, fresh off finishing in the top fifty in the country the previous year, I flew to Arizona for a Spartan Race that I was sure I was going to place well in. I didn't take the fact that it was a brutal race in the desert seriously and that I'd be running shortly after a six-hour flight. It was extremely irresponsible of me to ignore these factors. My ignorance of the facts of the situation left me overconfident and underprepared, and it showed in my results. I ran awfully in that race, dragging my feet and embarrassed the entire way.

I wrote myself the following brutally honest note after the race:

You finished in fifty-fifth place. Remember this feeling. Stop training to finish, and start training to win. Do more, try harder, and stop pitying yourself because the training hurts. Push past your exhaustion.

I needed to be honest with myself in order to fix the issue and not blame the elements that I hadn't prepared for. The problem wasn't the desert, it was that I did no research into what it took to run in this particular climate, and, as a consequence, I failed to prepare properly. Because I was honest with myself after my failure, I trained differently, harder, and smarter over the next few months. As a result, I won my first three races over the next twelve months—the Men's Health and Fitness City Challenge once and the Merrell Down & Dirty Obstacle Race twice. I also earned second place in the Men's Health Urbanathlon. I never thought I'd win these races in my wildest dreams, but honesty and hard work changed my path to get there.

During this time period, I had another honest moment with myself, in this case regarding my work life. At this point, I was still working in a mortgage division that provided no fulfilment. I stayed there out of comfort, not because the job was helping me to grow. I had reached a level of financial security that had caused me to become complacent. I can tell you with full confidence that money or wealth alone will not make you happy—I was miserable at my job every day. Because of that, I threw myself harder into those Spartan Races, training twice a day and spending more of my "working hours" researching how to get better at training than doing my actual job. Predictably, my production suffered. This trickled down to my staff, too.

No amount of winning races was addressing my main issue—that I was working eight hours a day in a place of complacency and comfort and that I hated it. Eventually, I was honest with myself and thought, "Hey Ralph. You are totally screwing this up. You're failing yourself and those around you." I woke up, changed my attitude, and eventually made changes to my business and daily routines. Mentally, physically, and financially, these changes benefited me and those around me. It didn't happen overnight, but by being honest with myself, I was able to change my path and pursue a new long-term goal of creating a better version of who I am.

One significant change to my business strategy I made was becoming a more public figure. I had always been someone who stayed behind the scenes until this moment. In general, I'm shy, and I don't like attracting attention. But I know that if I could build my brand, my business would grow in tandem. I started focusing on using video and social media to highlight my experiences, successes, and failures. At first, I was bad at it, and the process felt awkward. I'd make a video in which I gave tips about buying a home, and it would take me hours since I kept stumbling over my words, speaking too quickly, or cursing out of frustration. But over time, I got better and better. I'm proud to say that since opening myself up to the public eye, I've been quoted in several major publications, such as the *New York Times, The Wall Street Journal, Forbes*, and *USA Today*. I've even been featured on major networks as such MSNBC, Fox Business, and ABC. By becoming the public face of my business, I've brought in thousands of opportunities to those who have worked with me and are in my network. It turned out that my story was more interesting than I'd thought, and I only needed to develop the confidence to tell it.

Recognizing that you're in a growth trap is only the first step to climbing out of it. You need to *diagnose* the problem and understand what, exactly, you need to change in your particular situation. Often, the problem is that, even if you're working hard, you are simply on the wrong path. In this case, the three questions to ask yourself are: What am I naturally great at doing? Am I operating my life in the present, or am I stuck in the past or imagining how great things will be in the future without doing anything today? Am I being brutally honest with myself? By aligning your career with your natural talents, living in the present, and looking at yourself in the mirror with honesty, you can change your life's trajectory for the better.

Takeaways

- An underappreciated key to growth is knowing when to end or change your path when you realize that it's the wrong one for you. One kind of growth trap is getting stuck in a rut of daily efforts that, while they may be effective, are taking you down the wrong path. To honestly analyze whether or not you are on the right path, you need to ask yourself a few questions.
- The three questions to ask yourself are: 1) What am I naturally great at doing? 2) Am I operating my life in the present, or am I stuck in the past or imagining how great things will be in the future without doing anything today? 3) Am I being brutally honest with myself?
- Figure out where your talents and passions overlap and make that into your career.

Chapter Nine

Following a Plan

I n previous chapters, we have discussed developing the right habits, holding yourself accountable through those habits, and finding accountability partners. Habits and accountability partners are great, but at some point, we have to put our plan into action on our own. If you talk to most people, they will tell you that they can prepare their plan between fifty and seventy-five percent of the way, but they never truly feel ready to take the ultimate plunge to finalize their plan and execute it.

Here's the hard truth. We are never going to feel ready to grow. We are never going to feel fully equipped to implement our plan, become better versions of ourselves, and escape the growth trap. You're never totally ready, but that doesn't justify never starting.

I have learned through trial and error, reading books, and conversations with leaders in my business that implementing a mature plan takes the pressure off you. As a result, executing the process that propels your growth, success, and forward movement becomes much easier.

Now that we have an idea of how to form good habits and hold ourselves accountable, it's time to talk about making a plan and put it into action. Over the years, I've had many frustrating conversations with people who tell me their seemingly great ideas, but then they never take the steps to bring their ideas to fruition. I can tell that they'll never get their ideas off the ground by the fact that they have no action plan. A brilliant idea is only the first step—the immediate next question is always, "But then how do you activate it?"

When we are finally ready to show our plan to others and/or act on it, we instinctively start to feel stressful, fearful, and anxious. I believe that those three emotions have a direct correlation with growth. Counterintuitively, when we are under the weight of these emotions, we are likely growing the most.

The Six-Month Plan

To take action, we have to first decide what our goal is, then establish a long-term plan in order to achieve it, and finally move toward that goal over time. As we act on that plan, we will have short-term setbacks, failures, and moments of doubt. We may even lose faith that we can reach the goal at all. All of this is normal. Such feelings are part of the process that is our long-term plan. The long-term plan is a repeatable strategy that is imperative for avoiding the growth trap and advancing forward, like a recipe that yields good results every time—if you stick to it.

What has worked for me throughout my career is creating a six-month plan. Six months is not so long that my daily, weekly, and monthly schedule are negatively impacted, and it's not so short that small setbacks and failures will compromise the mission. To make a long-term plan successful, we need to learn what works for us and what doesn't and adjust accordingly as we grow toward success.

My first step in creating any of my long-term plans is to set a date and timeframe for completion. I can't stress enough how important this part of the process is. When I set a date for my plan, it forces me to take action rather than procrastinating. All of my great successes have had a set date so that I could work overtime toward that goal before the date arrived. This also leaves me time to fail, recognize what I did wrong, pivot, and continue down the path toward my long-term goal.

Birth of a Disruptor

I've always had a passion for mentoring others, and I'd come to be quite effective at it. Around 2018 I was encouraged to create a Mastermind class to teach others the methods I implemented to become successful. So I started to research, read about Mastermind classes, and even peruse other mentors' old classes. I spent my own money to learn about something I thought I was already doing. Unfortunately, none of the content that I consumed gave me a clear vision about what I should share with others in my own class.

My long-term goal became creating a Mastermind class no matter what. I made this a six-month plan for the reasons I gave earlier. The first class I started outlining was based on real estate investing, which I have a lot of experience with. But once I got into writing up the class content, I didn't see any unique value that separated my class from others in the field. Two months into my six-month plan, with chapters written and video filmed, I decided to scrap my plan completely and start over. Failing at my first plan and quickly recognizing my need to pivot was part of the long-term process, and I accepted this with no hesitation. You should never keep hammering down on a concept or plan that is not working. As long as you're still working toward your long-term goal, don't be afraid to change direction and make adjustments.

Shortly after I went back to the drawing board, I figured out what made my path to success unique. Compared with others in my field at the time, I was leveraging social media far more heavily in order to create a funnel of income for my business in mortgages and real estate. This is how I came up with my new concept of the Real Estate Disruptor. This would be the central idea of my new Mastermind class. In my class, I'd explain how to leverage marketing strategies that would be effective in any industry, not just real estate. Such marketing would grow your personal brand, raise your profile, build your network, and increase your income.

Four months to go.

As I started to think through how I'd explain my concept of a disruptor, I realized that I didn't do all of my brand-building on my own. I had a lot of help along the way. How would I work all of those people into my Mastermind course? That is how the idea was born to have the Mastermind class as a live event and bring everyone together for one day. The word "disrupt" is defined as, "to interrupt (an event, activity, or process) by causing a disturbance or problem." [1] The disturbance that I wanted to cause was to show mortgage and real estate professionals how to think outside the box when it came to branding themselves.

I had succeeded in branding myself by working and hiring high-level marketers outside of my businesses in mortgage and real estate. I had wanted to learn techniques that I wasn't seeing on a daily basis. This is another key you need for a long-term plan: to be willing to think outside the box and do something that you haven't done before.

---

1   https://disruptnow.org/#:~:text=Disruption% 20% E2% 80% 93% 20Disrupt% 20% 28v% 29% 20% 3A% 20to% 20interrupt% 20% 28an,drastically% 20alter% 20or% 20destroy% 20the% 20structure% 20of% 20% 28something% 29

Ambitious people set a big goal that they can reach but that never seemed possible through their previous short-term plans. As I've emphasized before, being uncomfortable and continuously changing is crucial for growth.

First Real Estate Disruptor conference, June 2019

The next step in building your plan is figuring out how you'll need to leverage your network in order to execute. For my Disruptors event, I needed activators to turn my vision into reality. Activators have been a huge part of my success. For this step of creating the process that will take you to your long-term goal, write down the people you have in your network who can be an asset in making sure the relevant tasks get done. Also, reach out to those who have experience and/or could serve as advisors on your path toward your goal. During lengthy projects, you'll need people around you who carry a positive attitude and can be transparent with you about whether or not your initial plans seem to be taking you toward your long-term goal.

For my long-term plan of hosting my Disruptors event, I needed three people: someone to help me on the creative side, a consistent and reliable backbone to help me handle the tasks that I couldn't pay attention to as I worked as leader on this project, and an activator to organize and promote the event to untapped networks.

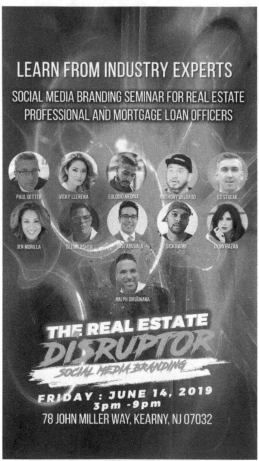

The beginning of Disruptor

Eulogio, my co-creator of the Real Estate Disruptor Program, has an incredibly creative mind, and so he played the role of creative director to make sure that the visuals of the event were perfect. He ensured that the video was inclusive of all the techniques that we had learned through our own processes of building our brands. He also would be a speaker at the event, where he'd tell the crowd about his own path to success.

Meagan, who had worked her way through the ranks starting at the age of twenty-one, had been with me for eight years at the time of our Real Estate Disruptors event. She would continue to be my backbone and serve as my activator by overseeing my daily mortgage business while I was busy preparing for the event. Another key to a long-term plan is for the network that you leverage to be consistent, predictable, and reliable. If you can understand where your people will be and how they will respond, and if you can rely on them to respond as you would, you will enjoy the peace and security necessary to focus on your plan. That's what Meagan has always been for me. She's a reliable person whom I gladly trusted with my daily operations while I spent my time working on our event. I also trained Meagan from day one, so the only business practices that she knew were those I taught her. This meant that I knew I could trust her to act in my stead while my attention was elsewhere.

The third person in my long-term crew was Vicky. She was someone who was very well networked. Vicky had been quite proactive in networking through her career, having become a member and/or participant at many chambers of commerce, cultural societies, and networking groups. As part of your long-term plan, it is always wise to grow your circle of influence or acquire partners who can do it for you. At some point, you will need to access the influence, knowledge, or advice from other specialists, and the type of network that Vicky had amassed was critical to the growth of my plan. She would drive the business and opportunities through her network, and I would "seal the deal" to fill our needs.

And so, the core of our team consisted of four specialized individuals. Together, we would complete the plan to get two hundred disruptors into my first-ever seminar for a significant entry fee.

Three months to go.

The scope and scale of my first seminar were very ambitious, and if I had known what I know now, I probably wouldn't have gone through with it. Funnily enough, ignorance of obstacles can often be a blessing in disguise. Sometimes we just have to ask what we feel we deserve and chase our gut instinct, regardless of how steep the mountain in front of us might be. Looking back, whenever I summoned the courage to reach beyond my capabilities, I've been pleasantly surprised at the benefits that have come after the fact. Not everyone will buy into your ambitions. However, every person who *does* is a win for you and your growth. Ask for what you deserve, and the reward is growth.

I had to ask myself three key questions to reach my long-term goal of hosting a successful event. The first was, "What problem am I trying to solve with my plan?" My answer was straightforward: to provide knowledge of my branding experience to industry members and to form lasting business relationships with them. But this question applies to the pursuit of any long-term goal, not just to my own. For your given problem, make the general question above more specific to you. For example, if you want to live a healthier life, you should ask yourself "How do I solve the problem of my fitness and diet?" If you want to reach a better position at work, ask "How do I make a plan to advance?" The list goes on. Maybe you want a better relationship with your spouse or children, so you'd set out to make a plan to be more patient and available to them. In general, when you're looking to solve a problem, decide what your goal is and then develop a plan of execution.

The second question I asked myself was, "Who are my strategic partners, and what is their incentive to follow the plan?" Our event ended up with around eight speakers that day, in addition to Eulogio and me. It was a mixture of good friends who were willing to do me a favor and individuals I had either worked with before on branding or those who I wanted to work with in the future. With one exception, every speaker would become a business partner of mine over the next few years. I forged new relationships that ultimately helped my business. Again, having the right people in your circle is invaluable, and the key is to match the right people to the problem that you're trying to solve. For the Disruptors conference, the people I chose as speakers would not only build a relationship with me, but they also opened themselves up to relationships with the two hundred attendees. I found partners who valued networking as much as I do. This is a practical strategy that will work in any field: find people who have a vision similar to yours, who want to grow with you, and who are eager to share access to their networks with you.

The third question I asked myself was, "What message or value am I bringing that solves the problem at hand and helps me grow?" For my event, the answer was, "Hey, let's brand together so we can grow our businesses and relationships in harmony." I would tell everyone at the conference about the mistakes I made, how I overcame them, who helped me do it, what I learned from the processes, and how I am using my network in the present to grow and add to my success.

One month to go.

The last thirty days of my plan were stressful, anxious, and full of obstacles. I had to make sure all the speakers were booked, the venue was properly equipped, our video technology was in order—and I had to market the hell out of the event. Oh, and we just had to sell two hundred tickets. No big deal! I can tell you that I wildly underestimated the complexity of my plan. However, because I had put a specific date on it and made personal and financial commitments, I had no choice but to pull it off. My back was against the wall, and it was the best place I could be. I *placed* my back against the wall, I wasn't forced there. Because I forced myself into a situation in which I had to plan, I didn't come into the event unprepared. This is something that is imperative to your plan, as well as to your journey toward growth and success: be *proactive* in putting your back against the wall in order to force growth, not be *reactive* by allowing something else to put you in a tough spot.

The day of the event finally came. If I said it did not go smoothly, that would be a massive understatement. The event started off well. It was a perfect late spring/early summer day, and because the event was on a rooftop, we enjoyed an amazing backdrop. But the catered food was late, as was the bartender. Most of the video crew flew in that day and was setting up only as I arrived. Meanwhile, the guests were already pouring in. My cohost was still getting her makeup done while half the crowd was already there and ready to go. The projector and screen weren't working; you couldn't make out any of the visuals because we didn't account for the sun being so strong in the direction of our cameras. Inside I was panicked, frustrated, and stressing out. But, fortunately for me, everybody was happy to be there on that beautiful day, the speakers got up and told wonderful stories about their professional growth, and it was exactly what the network of people came to see. I made amazing connections that day that I still have. No one knew about the problems we were having, because we remained calm as a team, did our jobs, and worked past the problems. Our crew of about ten did the work of fifty people that day. Because of our inexperience in planning a seminar, we were understaffed and overwhelmed. But as a team, we pulled together with the right people to get it done and built bonds that still serve us today.

This event was a springboard for multiple events that we would host over the next few years, which helped me build my business and my Real Estate Disruptor community even further. There are now thousands of members of what has been rebranded as the Disruptors Network. To this day, the Disruptors Network is in full force. It's founded on three principles that so much of the real estate industry has moved away from: passion, purpose, and positive impact. Our Disruptors Network breaks down the barriers in real estate by bringing together entrepreneurs in this space, both established and up-and-coming. And we offer more than in-person events now. I'm proud to say that the Disruptors Network offers podcasts, a docu-series, and a Disruptor Academy that educates young entrepreneurs about how to lead, overcome, inspire, and scale their business. Our video library offers Disruptor Network members cutting edge content that anyone in the real estate industry would love to access. Our docu-series highlights successful entrepreneurs who started out with nothing but succeeded because of their strong work ethic and perseverance. The Disruptors Network will continue to grow, solve problems, and make a mark on the world.

And it all started with my long-term plan to build a Mastermind class. A simple goal—though not an *easy* one—resulted in my personal growth, my team's growth, my network growth, and a whole new business strategy that continues to serve me to this day. One successful six-month plan has taught me lessons that I continue to use for all my long-term planning.

Takeaways

- We are never going to feel ready to grow. We are never going to feel fully equipped to implement our plan and escape the growth trap. Still, that doesn't justify never starting.
- To take action, we have to first decide what our goal is, then establish a long-term plan in order to achieve it, and finally move toward that goal over time. As we act on that plan, we will have short-term setbacks, failures, and moments of

doubt. We may even lose faith that we can reach the goal at all. All of this is normal.

- During your long-term plan, don't be afraid to pivot and make adjustments if something isn't working. For me, I went from planning a Mastermind class to hosting a two-hundred-person live event, and it was one of the best professional decisions I'd ever made.

- Figure out how to leverage your network in order to execute your plan. Without the help of my valuable colleagues such as Eulogio, Meagan, and Vicky, I never would've pulled off our event.

- At the start of your plan, ask yourself three questions: 1) What problem am I trying to solve? 2) Who are my strategic partners, and what is their incentive to follow the plan? 3) What value do I bring to the table that helps me solve the problem at hand?

- Be *proactive* in putting your back against the wall in order to force growth, not *reactive* by allowing something else to put you in a tough spot.

- Find a community of entrepreneurs in which everyone is eager to help each other through education, motivation, and networking.

Chapter Ten

How to Choose the Hard Road

P ursuing only goals that are easy to accomplish is one of the greatest obstacles to growth. The easy road doesn't push back or disagree with us. It lets us by without a fight. An easy workout, an easy challenge, or an easy assignment does nothing for the development of our character, our mind, our body, or our career. I guarantee that no effortless task will produce any personal growth or progress. The hard road, on the other hand, forces us to grow. Through challenge, we become better, smarter, faster, and more capable of overcoming future adversity. The hard road doesn't care about our feelings or who we think we may be. It just wants to stop us from accomplishing what we are striving for. The hard road will make us better every single day that we choose to go down it.

I have always hated running, which makes no sense given what I have accomplished as a runner. The reason that I continue to run three or four times a week is because I'm not great at it, and it challenges me every single time I do it. Running makes me uncomfortable, which, as we've discussed in earlier chapters, forces me to improve both mentally and physically. Doing something we are good at all the time is too easy. The reason we don't mind taking the easy path is precisely *because* it's so comfortable. However, this is also why an easy task or routine gets boring very quickly. Being great at *anything* over long enough stretches will get boring.

One of my long-term goals is to remain physically healthy and fit for as long as my body will allow it. I know that running is an activity that I'll be able to continue doing as I get older. It helps keep me in top condition. It's also something that allows me to clear my mind. When I go out for a run, I have no ability to think about the other stresses of my life, because I'm too focused on trying mentally to get myself through something I don't totally enjoy. While running itself is brutal for me, I *always* feel mentally and physically euphoric after I'm finished. Whenever I'm engaged in a difficult or unpleasant task, I always keep the end result in mind. In this case, this is both the feeling and health benefits that running gives me.

Short-Term Pain or Long-Term Suffering

Life fools us into thinking we have choices. Let's take running as an example again. Go ask anyone who's run a marathon but didn't finish. I guarantee that they hit that wall at eighteen or twenty miles and decided to quit, instead of pushing through to the finish line. And I'm sure they felt relieved to do so. That first breath we take when we stop doing something that is causing pain or stress is the greatest breath of relief we can experience. However, this short-term relief is an illusion, as it assumes that the pain is over once you quit. Ask those same runners how they felt the next day, when they saw all of the pictures and results of people who *did* finish the race. The mental pain that they will feel for years—unless they do something to resolve it—is so much worse than the pain it would have taken for them to finish. Quitting a challenge always becomes a painful memory. And in the long run, it can become a crippling habit.

This tradeoff has led me to conclude that we don't, in fact, have a choice in the matter. We *must* do the hard thing every time, if we really want to grow. Repeatedly making the wrong, easy choice can be the main cause of remaining stagnant in life. We have so many options in everyday life between easy and hard roads. Some of them are simple: should I go to bed early so I can wake up and exercise, or should I stay up late, eat snacks, scroll through social media, and watch Netflix? Should I spend time with my family, or should I go out to drink after work for three hours? Do I read a book that will help me improve my skills or play video games? We all know that none of the mindless, easy activities mentioned above will improve our lives, and I guarantee that they don't fit into any of our long-term plans.

Are you willing to make the hard choices to make yourself grow? To be sure, this doesn't mean you have to give up everything that is fun or easy; it just means that you have to make the right decisions that lead toward your growth. Some of that is definitely going to be hard. When it comes down to it, are you willing to do what's difficult so that you can reap the reward in the future? Our only real choice is to continuously improve our chosen set of skills by getting uncomfortable. As you know by now, we can only break out of growth traps and reach our goals by pushing through discomfort and taking the hard road.

Making Our Brains Work in Our Favor

Taking the hard road is our best option. But how do we ensure that we succeed in doing so? There's a reason that so many of us choose to eat junk food, phone it in at work, and generally cut corners in life, even though we know that we shouldn't be doing any of those things. What strategies can we employ to help make the challenging road easier to take?

Dr. Judson Brewer, a Yale psychiatrist, neuroscientist, and *New York Times* bestselling author, has theorized that there are surprisingly simple ways to break bad habits and replace them with the right habits. Brewer discusses one of the most evolutionarily conserved learning processes in the brain known in science: the reward-based learning process (this means that this process has remained unchanged for an enormous number of generations). This is also known as positive and negative reinforcement. It consists of three sequential steps: trigger, behavior, and reward. Each time this process is implemented, we learn to repeat the cycle due to the reward mechanism. The more we engage in a given cycle, the more the behavior becomes instilled as a habit. For example, when we see food that looks good, our minds are triggered to eat the food, then we act on that impulse, and then we feel good as a reward. We integrate a context-dependent memory into our minds and unconsciously seek to repeat the process the next time we experience the same trigger.

Dr. Brewer argues that, often, when we are trying to establish a new habit, we are actually *fighting* this reward-based learning process. Instead, we should *take advantage* of it—in other words, we should develop new habits by leaning into our inborn psychology, rather than trying to resist them.

"What if instead of fighting our brains or trying to force ourselves to pay attention, we instead tapped into this natural reward-based learning process?" Dr. Brewer asked in a TED talk that has been viewed more than ten million times on YouTube.[2]

---

2   "A Simple Way to Break a Bad Habit | Judson Brewer." n.d. Www.youtube. com. Accessed February 25, 2022. https://www.youtube.com/watch?v=-moW9jvvMr4&t=288s.

Our brains are known for utilizing cognitive control. This means that we use cognition to control our behavior. Understanding what we get from our habits and how they develop helps us to control and even replace them. Also, understanding how we ended up with bad habits gives us a good reason to not shame ourselves for bad behavior. For example, in the same TED talk, Dr. Brewer gives the example of people who are addicted to smoking. In his own research, he asked smokers to "go ahead and smoke, just be really curious what it's like when you do." The smokers realized how disgusting the habit was and moved from "knowledge to wisdom"—before practicing mindfulness, of course the smokers all knew that smoking was bad for them. But after actively thinking about smoking while engaging in the behavior, they came to know it in their bones. This disrupts the brain's trigger-behavior-reward process, since now the reward of feeling good after a cigarette has been "broken."

On the other side of the coin, how can we exploit our brain's circuitry to establish positive habits? In the context of the reward-based learning process, we should think of the *end result* as a reward and the *painful process* as the behavior. By working to implement this cycle, we can develop new habits far more easily than we could by simply "willing" ourselves to go down the hard road. Also, the more we reorient the reward-based learning process in our favor, the less interested we will be in engaging in bad habits in the first place.

This is what mindfulness is all about: seeing clearly the lack of results when we get caught up in counterproductive behaviors, becoming disenchanted with our current, "easy" path, and making the choice to do something about it. This won't happen overnight, but as we see the results of our newfound behaviors, we gradually let go of old habits and form new ones.

Get Out of Your Own Way

Dr. Brewer believes that you are already awesome, you just need to get out of your own way. But what does that mean, exactly?

Lolo Jones was a top female American hurdler going into the 2008 Beijing Olympics. Everything was going according to plan on her path to Olympic gold. In the final of the one-hundred-meter hurdle, she was in the lead and in what she describes as an almost complete out-of-body calm. But toward the end of the race, she started to consciously think about making sure she didn't hit the hurdles. "Make sure my legs are snapping out," she told herself. And just like that, she hit the next hurdle and lost. She visualized a negative outcome instead of letting her natural state of mind take over, which may have directly resulted in her losing the gold.

Jones' mental clarity before her mind was cluttered with thoughts is what Brewer describes as *flow state*. This is a mental state in which a person is fully immersed, present, and feels an almost magically energized focus. Flow is a hallmark of extraordinary performance. Whether it is Michael Jordan scoring fifty points in a basketball game, or someone rising to a challenge that they never thought they would be able to handle, flow state is the name of the game if you want to excel.

Dr. Brewer has outlined several common ways in which we get in our own way. He argues that getting into flow state allows us to overcome distracted thinking and resist our own bodily sensations so that we can perform optimally in whatever situation we find ourselves in. When we fail to master our body and mind, the result is what happened to Lolo Jones. Dr. Brewer admits that acquiring the flow state is not straightforward. We can all "take flow" in fleeting moments in our lives, but how can we learn to get into it at the drop of a hat? Answer: by paying attention. What is life like when we avoid getting caught up in thinking? When we get out of our own way, we are happier, more engaged with the world, and more compassionate. As a result of all of this, we end up performing our best. The key is to get out of our own way when we choose the hard road. And that is what Dr. Brewer means when he says that we are already awesome.[3]

I get out of my own way by always focusing on my long-term reward. If I work out, it's to feel better *after* the exercise routine. I've become addicted to the feeling I get when I'm finished, even though I know how poorly I'll feel at the beginning. This holds true for all of my long-term goals: I focus on what's at the end and not what I'll have to undergo to get there. I think of how accomplished and happy I'm going to feel with the end result. That's how I get through hard tasks. I've come to appreciate that when I'm going through something easy, it's probably not going to help me achieve any of my long-term goals.

So, the next time you're faced with a choice between the easy path and the hard road, remember how fulfilled you'll be after choosing the latter. Do this at every fork in the road. Gradually, it will become second-nature, and you will find that you get out of your own way for the rest of your life.

Takeaways

- Pursuing only goals that are easy to accomplish is one of the greatest obstacles to growth. I guarantee that no effortless task will produce any personal growth or progress. The hard road, on the other hand, forces us to grow. The hard road will make us better every single day that we choose to go down it.

- The mental pain that those who quit a marathon will feel for years is so much worse than the pain it would have taken for

---

3   "You're Already Awesome. Just Get out of Your Own Way!: Judson Brewer MD, Ph.D. At TEDxRockCreekPark." n.d. Www.youtube.com. Accessed February 25, 2022. https://www.youtube.com/watch?v=jE1j5Om7g0U.

them to finish. Quitting a challenge always becomes a painful memory. And in the long run, it can become a crippling habit. Always remember that the short-term pain of pursuing challenges is always less severe than the memory of having quit.

- Dr. Brewer argues that often when we are trying to establish a new habit, we are actually *fighting* our brain's reward-based learning process of experiencing a trigger, engaging in a behavior, and then receiving a mental reward. Instead, we should *take advantage* of it—in other words, we should develop new habits by leaning into our inborn psychology, rather than trying to resist it. We should turn difficult tasks into learned behaviors and know that the reward will be reaching our desired long-term outcomes.

- Dr. Brewer has outlined several common ways in which we get in our own way. He argues that getting into flow state allows us to overcome distracted thinking and resist our own bodily sensations so that we can perform optimally in whatever situation we find ourselves in. Brewer admits that acquiring the flow state is not straightforward. We can all "take flow" in fleeting moments in our lives, but how can we learn to get into it at the drop of a hat? By paying attention.

- What is life like when we avoid getting caught up in thinking? When we get out of our own way, we are happier, more engaged with the world, and more compassionate. As a result of all of this, we end up performing our best. The key is to get out of our own way when we choose the hard road. And that is what Dr. Brewer means when he says that we are already awesome.

Chapter Eleven–

Fight or Flee

My Mother, the Protector

The definition of "fear" is "a distressing emotion aroused by impending danger, evil, pain, etc., whether the threat is real or imagined."[4] From a young age, I knew exactly what fear was. My mother, Joanne, is the sweetest woman you'll ever meet in your life. There is not a bad bone in her body. Growing up, I was the baby of the family and very close to my mom. When I didn't get into preschool—it was a lottery system—my mom chose not to return to work and instead stay home with me. We spent a year together, watching TV, playing games, and just hanging around each other.

Even though I was only four years old, I remember that time very well. My mom was my protector. She never wanted anything bad to happen to me. And she was the person who introduced me to the concept of fear through her many life lessons. Some of them were useful,

---

4   "Definition of Fear | Dictionary.com." 2016. Www.dictionary.com. 2016. https://www.dictionary.com/browse/fear.

like "don't touch the hot stove" or "don't run into the street" or "don't put that in your mouth." But some of them convinced me that I was only safe when I was with her. To this day, my mom takes my side no matter what I've done. God forbid anyone would have anything bad to say about me—let alone do something to me—because my mom is the first person in line to defend me.

I talked in previous chapters about the work ethic, discipline, consistency, and sense of fearlessness my father taught me. From my mom, I learned how to be a protector and the importance of helping others, no matter what they've done to me. My mom instilled in me a desire to make everyone around me feel safe and happy.

Fighting Your Fear

Growing up in my New York neighborhood, I learned the meaning of "fight-or-flee" very early on, and not through reading about it. Fight-or-flee is that thought in your mind, right before you confront something that's scaring you. This is a survival instinct that evolution has given us, as science has shown.[5] You make a quick decision to attack or run. This instinct doesn't only kick in when you're facing a literal fight. Anything could trigger a fight-or-flee response. It could be something as harmless as writing down your thoughts, which might terrify you. It could be continuing to run down the road, even when you're out of breath. Fight-or-flee shows up in every domain in life and has been a theme in my life for a long time.

People will rarely admit this, but fear dominates many of our lives. Fear of loss. Fear of failure. Fear of being alone. Fear of never succeeding. They live their life in a constant state of fear over losing

---

5   "Understanding the Stress Response." 2011. Harvard Health. March 1, 2011.
     https://www.health.harvard.edu/staying-healthy/understanding-the-stress-
     response#:~:text=A%.

something they don't even know whether or not they want. Being aware of actual dangers is necessary for our survival, but living in a constant state of "flee" will never get us anywhere we want to go. To avoid getting caught in the growth trap of "flee," you have to learn to accept fear and fight through it. I've had to learn this lesson in every stage of life and in my career. Hell, I'm still learning that today.

Ralph's parents and children, 2021

Choosing to Fight over Running Away

When Curtis "50 Cent" Jackson was shot nine times early in his music career over a beef in his neighborhood, he headed for intense physical rehabilitation. He made a couple critical choices during that time to help him fight fear moving forward. For example, he moved into a house near where he had been shot, and he underwent rehab there. For those who don't know about New York City, he lived in Jamaica, Queens. You could move five miles away into a neighboring borough, and it'd be like you were moving from California to Idaho. That's how different New York City neighborhoods are from each other. If you moved from one borough to another, no one would ever be able to find you.

But Jackson went right back to his old neighborhood. He did this because he knew that if he didn't face his fear and go back, he would always suffer from the fear of being chased and killed for the rest of his life. Now, this is obviously an extreme case, but that mentality of facing bullies, competitors, adversaries, and detractors has been the calling card of his career and the catalyst of his successes. Jackson is also known now for his famous TV show *Power* on the Starz network. He just re-signed a deal with them for more than one-hundred-and-fifty million dollars.

What most people don't know is that Jackson had a show on MTV first, called *The Money and the Power*, which failed and was cancelled after one season. Instead of quitting TV forever, he decided to fight and pitch a new show, *Power*. Starz, the only network that was interested, offered him only seventeen thousand dollars per episode to write, produce, and act in the show. He literally could've made ten times as much money going to a club and doing an appearance. But he took the deal, bet on himself, and the rest is history. Fight or flee. What if he had fled and left his home after he was shot? Maybe he would have still been successful, or maybe not. Regardless, who he is today is shaped by that moment, and he continues to hold that same attitude in every aspect of his life.

A Childhood of Earning Respect

In an odd way, I can relate to 50 Cent. Where I grew up in my Brooklyn neighborhood, there were a lot of quiet, hardworking people. But there was a certain element of survival of the fittest, and you couldn't be a pushover if you wanted to succeed. One of the bloodiest mob wars in history took place between 1991 and 1993—on the very corner streets and spaces of my own neighborhood. When it was over, there had been a significant amount of death, mayhem, and panic throughout Brooklyn, and especially in my neighborhood of Dyker Heights. I was finishing out my years in junior high school while the mob violence became an everyday reminder that we had to carry ourselves in such a way that we couldn't be pushed around. This element was mixed in with the blue collar mentality of Dyker Heights. Some of the lessons I learned there would've taken me decades to learn in business, because when pride, reputation, and survival are on the line, people will show you their true colors immediately. In business, it can take someone years to reveal their true identity. I'm not saying any of my childhood experiences are ideal or recommended, but I do appreciate how they shaped my character.

Besides my mother, my brother Michael was my other protector. He was also the person who taught me how to fight and protect myself, mostly because I was always defending myself from him messing with me!

On my fortieth birthday, my loved ones put together a tribute book for me. In it, Mike told the following story:

"Ralph has always been a fighter and a leader. When we were kids, I always wanted to make sure that every mistake I made, he'd be able to avoid. But he was tough and always carved out his own path. I remember when he was about ten years old, my mom would let me take Ralph to the schoolyard to play sports with the big kids (I was three years older). He was a natural-born athlete and was always able to compete with those above his age. Now, he can compete with those below his age! Roller hockey was a big neighborhood competition between kids of all ages, some older than both of us. We'd come in and play games all day. Ralph was out the first day of the season, and some of the kids were trying to bully him. I lost it, and when I chased them with a hockey stick, they took off. I was momentarily feeling prideful that I came to his aid. That lasted about a second before Ralph began screaming at me, telling me he could fight his own battles and that he didn't need my help. He got back to it and played some great hockey. I learned that day he would never need me, or anyone else, to stand by him. I'm glad to have him by my side."

Although I don't remember that incident, I do remember carrying that general attitude for most of my youth. I was smaller than the other kids and was mostly a happy child, always smiling. But I didn't want to be taken advantage of. I learned that if I had a choice of fight-or-flee, I actually had *no* choice. No one will remember every time you stood up for what you believed in, but run away once, and it will follow you for the rest of your life.

At least, that's what it was like during my adolescence. I went to a neighborhood Catholic school, and we'd be let out thirty minutes before the local public school, specifically so that we could avoid conflict with them. We stuck out like a sore thumb with our proper uniforms. One day I was kept after school for detention, and by the time I got out, I was in the dead center of public school number 201's dismissal traffic. My friend and I were walking home when we were stopped by five boys from the public school who demanded our money and our bags.

Fight-or-flee.

My friend started to hand over everything he had, but I refused and challenged them to make me. It was surely not smart, because we were way outnumbered. Before I could get my head handed to me, though, someone came out of their home and told us to get out of there before she called the cops. Everyone ran—crisis averted.

When I ran into the leader of this group a few weeks later, he was in another potential scuffle with a neighborhood kid over a girl. When he saw me, he recognized me from our previous interaction. He pulled me aside and said, "This is what I heard this guy did with my girl-friend. What do you think?" I explained to him that that wasn't possible, because the kid had been upstate with his family and couldn't have done it. With a mutual respect now established, he took me at my word and moved on. This teenager would eventually become a man with bad habits and would be in and out of jail. At that time, we were just neigh-borhood kids at a crossroads, and my instincts told me that "fight" would be my best option to earn respect, which was everything to me.

As I advanced in life, I'd consistently learn about when "fight" was my best option, although the types of fights I experienced continued to change. When I moved to Staten Island at the age of fifteen, I was forced to make all new friends. Playing roller hockey in a new place for the first time, one of the neighborhood boys decided to test me, the new kid. Ronnie made some kind of comment and out of fear that I would lose respect I didn't even have yet in the new neighborhood, we came to blows. Afterward, we dusted ourselves off and finished the game. I ended up being the best man at Ronnie's wedding thirteen years later. He is one of my best friends to this day. That day, we had earned a mutual respect for each other. Fight-or-flee.

Left to right: Matt, Me, Big Mike, My brother Michael, Dominick, My dad Ralph

Big Mike

I met another one of my lifelong friends, Big Mike, around that same time. He was one of the two Mikes in our group. Our other friends were Matt, R.J., and the other Mike. We are all still friends. Big Mike was the largest, toughest, and most athletic of our group. What I learned from being around Mike in high school, college, and early adulthood was that we were going to protect each other, not follow others, and be ourselves. While Mike became one of the most feared people in our city as a teen because of his ability to fight and willingness to do it over and over again, that's not what I learned most from him. What he and the rest of the group taught me was the need to surround yourself with the right people and protect them at all costs. That is still important to me today and helps me avoid the growth trap of settling in the comfort of negative company. Your circle has to be those who have your best interests at heart and are not jealous or envious. Whenever one of us was in trouble or needed help, it was *all* of our problem, not just that person's. When I had a fight-or-flee moment for someone in my circle, again, I had no choice: it was always fight.

I still use these principles to this day. When creating a culture of growth around you, whether it's as a leader or part of a group, it's imperative that everyone has a one-for-all and all-for-one mind-set. That's no easy feat. But if anyone is willing to disrupt that culture, harm anyone, or stray from the principles of the group, that person has to go. Fight-or-flee: you either run away from confronting bad actors, or you take them head-on for the benefit of everyone else.

Mike eventually became a high level federal agent. He continues to protect those around him, only in different ways than he used to.

Tommy the Fighter

Later on in my career, I met a new business partner who is still with me today. Tommy came to me in 2012 as a leader in another mortgage company in need of a new home for him and his team. We clicked immediately. Tommy grew up in a similar neighborhood to mine, Howard Beach in Queens, and with a similar background. He was raised by a single mom and always had to fight to earn everything in his life. At thirteen, he went to work as a busboy at a local catering hall because his family needed the money. He would sometimes work until three in the morning, because his mom made the waiters promise to drive him home and make sure he was safe. At eighteen, he didn't have the choice of college—his grades were bad and his family didn't have enough savings—and he needed to make money to support his family, so he got an entry level job at a small Wall Street firm. While he was happy being there, he knew that this place wasn't Goldman Sachs and may not have been on the up-and-up. So he made as much as he could by working the phones twelve hours a day, saved up his money, and bought his first property that he planned to manage.

Ralph and Tommy at their barbershop, 2019

When the company ultimately went under, Tommy was left without a job again and resorted to the best option he had—manual labor. With no experience, he managed to talk his way into the carpenters' union. He needed to keep the money coming in, and he wanted to keep buying real estate. A few years after staying afloat in this way, a friend told Tommy about the mortgage business in 2005. This seemed like a great fit for his interest in real estate. So, over the next few years, Tommy rose to become the top salesperson in his company with no training and no favors—just his fight-and-never-flee attitude.

When the market crashed in 2008, Tommy was one of the few people in the mortgage business who had saved his money for a rainy day. That's when he pounced. While others—like me—were reeling and scrambling for jobs, Tommy was buying more real estate at huge discounts. He was running in when everyone else was running out because of his fight-or-flee attitude. Over the next five years, Tommy would amass an additional thirty properties, which are still part of his portfolio today and are worth about thirty times as much as when he purchased them. The reason I can't give you an exact valuation is because he never speaks about it. I had to piece this information together through almost ten years of conversations as business partners. He didn't do any of this for the glamour—it was always fight-or-flee. "My mom needs help with money, but I'm just a kid—doesn't matter, time to go to work," he'd think. "The world doesn't think I'm smart or good enough because I didn't go to college—doesn't matter, time to fight and prove them wrong." He finally started making money in mortgages, and the market crashed—didn't matter.

Tommy was never going to let the people around him suffer like he did, and he was always saving for a rainy day. And when the rain came, he had an umbrella. So he fought more and took advantage of opportunities that no one was just going to hand to him. Tommy never made excuses for himself or others. He just got up every day and fought. He is proof that if you fight, you can make it on your own.

Fight or flee.

Takeaways

- Fight-or-flee is that thought in your mind right before you confront something that's scaring you. You make a quick decision to attack or run. This instinct doesn't only kick in when you're facing a literal fight. Anything could trigger a fight-or-flee response. It could be something as harmless as writing down your thoughts, which might terrify you. It could be continuing to run down the road, even when you're out of breath.

- Most people will never admit this, but fear dominates their lives. Fear of loss. Fear of failure. Fear of being alone. Fear of never succeeding. Living in a constant state of "flee" will never get us anywhere we want to go. To avoid getting caught in the growth trap of "flee," you have to learn to accept fear and fight through it.

- If you have a choice of fight-or-flee, you actually have *no* choice. No one will remember every time you stood up for what you believed in, but run away once, and it will follow you for the rest of your life.

Chapter Twelve–

The Comeback

E veryone loves a good comeback. Witnessing someone rise, fall, and then rise again is so enjoyable that we've told tales of comebacks for thousands of years. It's understandable why we love them. To witness someone refuse to give up even after he or she has taken a hit inspires all of us that we can do the same.

Rocky Rises

One of my favorite movies of all time is *Rocky*—any *Rocky*. For those who don't know the beginnings of the Rocky story, he was a professional boxer who found some early success in the profession because he was born with natural ability. But, like most of us, he got caught in the growth trap and accepted failure instead of trying to grow intentionally. Eventually, considered past his prime, he lived as a street thug who worked as a loan shark. By a stroke of good fortune, he was chosen as the best fighter of his time for a championship belt match against Apollo Creed. Because of this dramatic opportunity, he woke up from his slumber and went into growth mode. When it came time for his fight, his determination met his inherent talent, and he gave the fight of a lifetime. He didn't win, but he gained an army of fans and a wealth of opportunities.

This is the anatomy of a great comeback. Caught in the growth trap, not reaching our potential, unhappy and stuck, we decide to make a drastic change, take a chance on ourselves, force growth, and make a comeback. Our comebacks may not make us famous, but they are essential for reaching our true potential and finding joy in what we do daily.

Every day is a chance to get up, grow, and improve. I have witnessed millions of comeback stories, from both watching the news and observing the people in my personal life. Sometimes they inspire and amaze us. Sometimes, you might harbor ill will or harsh judgments about the person who made a comeback. That feeling is usually more about your own path than about the person who just found success. The same applies when others judge *you* for *your* success. What we are experiencing then is a very superficial kind of hate, but the reality is that your detractors feel insecure and unaccomplished themselves, so they need to diminish your shine to rationalize their lack of it. We will come back to this in a little.

Napoleon's Return from Exile

In 1814, at the Congress of Vienna, Napoleon Bonaparte was exiled to Alba, off the coast of Italy. Even in jail, he loomed large. Those who had taken over his empire were still scared of him—so much so that they couldn't even kill him. In 1815, with a small faction of his former army supporting him, Napoleon escaped from Alba on a ship and headed back toward France. He could've gone anywhere, but he chose to go right back to the scene of the crime. Once there, he used his army to march on Paris to try to seize back control of his former empire. Instead of fearing him or feeling unhappy about his return, the people of France saw Napoleon as a figure who had been down-and-out but managed to valiantly come back. They embraced him as somebody they wanted as their leader. When he reached Paris, everybody surrounded him, joyous at his return. This is someone who had terrorized the country and had not been good for their well-being. And yet to see him return brought the people back to their days of glory. He got off the mat and started to inspire a nation again. The king who had replaced Napoleon even fled the country.

But Napoleon's second reign did not last very long. Within one hundred days, France was in complete disarray, and the enthusiasm of his new following diminished. Then their brief elation completely broke when he led them to war. At the Battle of Waterloo, he was defeated again. This time, he was exiled for good, sent to an island on the outskirts of Africa.

Napoleon's story shows us what to do and not to do when trying to make a comeback. Because France had not made any progress in his absence, the people had started to romanticize him as a leader. Knowing this—because of insider information—Napoleon was confident that he could inspire them and could get them to follow him once again. The problem was that he wasn't a changed man. He was the same destructive, power-hungry, insecure person he was before his first defeat. So when he came back, the people's celebration over his return didn't last. Our failures should teach us lessons that cause us to humble ourselves, learn, and evaluate our process before we make a comeback. I don't believe any failure is final, but if you don't learn from it, then you are doomed to fail again. This is rule number one in orchestrating a comeback following a fall from grace. Humble yourself, learn, and make the right changes so that you can do better next time. Learn from your failures and grow into a better you.

Another Boxer Named Tyson

Tyson Fury was born to be a boxer. His father literally named him after the famous boxer Mike Tyson. Standing six feet, nine inches, and almost three hundred pounds, he is as intimidating as he is skilled and charming. He was an accomplished amateur boxer in England and Ireland, and by the time he turned professional at the age of twenty, he had already won the prized American Boxing Federation (ABF) championship. His professional career started out great, with a 24–0 record, which set him up for a fight with the unified heavyweight champion of the world, the previously unbeatable Wladimir Klitschko. Fury won this fight by a unanimous decision. Now king of the boxing universe, you would think this would have been the greatest moment of Tyson's life.

But Tyson was using alcohol and drugs to cope with mental health struggles that were hiding beneath the surface. Two years later, more than one hundred pounds heavier than his previous fighting weight, Tyson was stripped of his heavyweight championship belt due to inactivity. After bouts of suicidal thoughts and more self-destruction, Tyson finally decided to get help for his psychological issues.

Over the next two years, he would bring both his brain and his body back to health. In 2018, after four years of inactivity, Tyson was finally comfortable in his fame and health, and he had discovered his true purpose. He came back to fight the champion at that time, Deontay Wilder. The fight ended in a controversial draw, although most thought he had won. Just a year later, Tyson knocked out Wilder to once again become heavyweight champion of the world.

Tyson not only came back as a fighter, but he also became a champion for mental health. He publically spoke about all of his issues: how he fell from grace and nearly destroyed himself, how he asked for help, and how he came back. He showed how others could do the same. He has since published two books about mental health and his mission to help others.

When Tyson got off the canvas and fought himself back to success, he gained millions of followers who supported him. He not only applied the first step in the comeback process—learning from our mistakes—but he showed us how to execute step two. That is, he recognized what caused him to fail, accepted it, and then worked to fix it. Because he was willing to accept what was causing his failure and make an effort to change, his comeback story has not only helped him but also millions of others dealing with the same issues.

The third and perhaps most important step in a comeback is to consistently grow without the need for approval or pats on the back from others. When you're down-and-out, you will find that people will sympathize, commiserate, and try to lift you up. Because you are not a threat to them in your depleted state, and you don't make them feel bad about themselves, they are comfortable helping you and trying to get you to accomplish your goals. When you start to win or make a comeback, some of those people will stick around and show joy as you reach new heights. Once your consistent growth and wins start to add up, however, ninety-five percent of those people will disappear. They will start to feel threatened and insecure that you are surpassing their expectations. Those responses shouldn't make you feel bad. In fact, the way they feel or act toward you has nothing to do with you. It mostly has to do with *their* failure to do as you did. Those people are stuck and unhappy. It is important to know this and not let it stop your own growth.

Climbing All Ladders at Once

Rich Sadiv is not only a friend but also someone who inspires me to be better, be more consistent, and become a greater version of myself. Rich was born to an immigrant family in New Jersey. By the time he was a young man in his twenties, he got a job at UPS working the nightshift, loading trucks for delivery using the work ethic his family had instilled in him. It was around this time that Rich found a new challenge in powerlifting. This is a strength sport that consists of three attempts to lift as much weight as possible in the squat, the bench press, and the deadlift. As in the sport of Olympic weightlifting, it involves the athlete attempting to lift the maximum weight of a barbell loaded with plates in a single lift effort. Outside of the Olympics, this is mostly an unknown sport. There is no money to be earned, no fame, and no TV or movie appearances for the star athletes. It's a small, very skilled community that has grown in popularity over the decades because of social media.

Rich not only ended up working his way up the corporate ladder at UPS from truck loader to corporate executive over a twenty-year career, but on a parallel track, he also became one of the best dead-lifting powerlifters in the entire world. If you saw Rich, you wouldn't think that he was a powerlifter at first sight. He has used that illusion to overwhelm many opponents in competitions. He has an unassuming build—six-foot-two and around one-hundred-and-ninety pounds, tall and lean. He doesn't look like a huge cartoon character you'd see in strongest man competitions on ESPN. Over his powerlifting career, he has achieved fourteen New Jersey state records, five national records, and one world record in the deadlift. He did it mostly in front of small audiences without recognition. This never stopped him from improving. When Rich was inducted into the powerlifting hall of fame recently, he accepted his prize but didn't make a big deal out of it. As a matter of fact, I had to ask him about it to even learn that this had happened.

When Rich decided to leave UPS and work full time at his own gym franchise, he attacked it with the same consistency and lack of fanfare. He even ran an NFL combine with Martin Rooney at his gym (an NFL combine is a weeklong event during which college football players perform physical and mental tasks in front of NFL scouts). He has helped to train over two-hundred-and-fifty NFL draft picks, which includes all-pros, Super Bowl champions, and Hall-of-Famers. He has done all of this with very little recognition. He is the man behind the scenes. He doesn't look for the approval of others. He is simply obsessed with being consistent and achieving bigger and bigger goals.

Rich Sadiv and I, 2018

You might wonder why I've included Rich's story, given that he's never made a comeback. But that's exactly why: he has worked so hard in life that he never took a significant step back in the first place. Rich has taught me that it is possible to *never* have to make a comeback, if you're willing to do what is necessary to move in only one direction: forward.

Now in his fifties, Rich is still one of the most consistent people I have ever met, and he continues to improve his fitness level, his business, and his quality of life with his better-for-myself attitude. He has accomplished all of his major life goals without the need or want for others to tell him that he's doing a great job. This is an imperative part of both the growth process and the mental process of creating fulfillment and self-love.

Takeaways

- Everyone loves a good comeback. To witness someone refuse to give up even after he or she has taken a hit inspires all of us that we can do the same.
- The anatomy of a great comeback is as follows: caught in the growth trap, not reaching our potential, unhappy and stuck, we decide to make a drastic change. Then we take a chance on ourselves, force growth, and begin a comeback. Our comebacks may not make us famous, but they are essential for reaching our true potential and finding joy in what we do daily.
- An important step in a comeback is to consistently grow without the need for approval or pats on the back from others.
- In principle, it is possible to *never* have to make a comeback, if you're willing to do what is necessary to move in only one direction: forward.

Chapter Thirteen–

Into the Future

I f we have learned anything from the 2020–2021 COVID-19 pandemic, it's that change is inevitable. If we want to avoid getting trapped by the constant changes in life, we need to become adaptable. I used to resist change. The mere thought of it gave me intense anxiety, and so I'd avoid it at all costs. Looking back, a lot of my growth traps were caused simply by my irrational resistance to change.

I've had a colorful career, full of ups and downs. Even now, after I've achieved a lot of professional and personal success, I often think about what's next for me. Now that I'm willing to adapt to change, when I consider my future, I think about the ever-changing landscape in my industry and how I can adjust to grow with it and take advantage of it.

Adapting by Telling Stories

Throughout history, some of the greatest success stories stemmed from overcoming a growth trap around change. Because of his innovative, ever-evolving style, Steve Jobs empowered himself to escape numerous growth traps. In 1983, after creating what he had thought was his greatest invention, the Lisa, he was fired and kicked out of his own company because it had failed so spectacularly. The Lisa was a personal desktop computer intended for business users. In order to advertise what he had thought was an amazing product, he'd taken out a nine-page ad in the *New York Times* to boast about The Lisa's supposed technological superiority. But nobody appreciated the product because it was too "geeky."

Frankly, Jobs himself didn't get it, either. Along with Steve Wozniak and Ronald Wayne, Jobs had founded Apple in 1976. Only four years later, the company went public, selling 4.6 million shares at twenty-two dollars each. Naturally, Jobs was feeling confident at the dawn of the eighties. He became convinced that all they needed to do to become the top company in the world was create products that were technologically superior to those of their competitors. This turned out to be one of his greatest miscalculations—although the Lisa was initially praised by the media and sold well, by the second half of 1984 sales drastically declined.

Steve Jobs ended up leaving Apple in September 1985, but his passion for technology propelled him forward. He joined a small company called Pixar, which many of us now recognize as the powerhouse responsible for almost every major animation breakthrough over the last three decades. They are the creators of *Toy Story* and other such amazing movies. At Pixar, Steve learned the art of storytelling.

In 1997, when Jobs returned to Apple, he brought his newfound knowledge of storytelling with him, and Apple skyrocketed to success because of it. The company's tradition of storytelling continues to this day. For example, they run a "Start Something New" initiative, in which they show off artistic creations that people have made using

Apple's products. In this way, Apple advertises its products by telling the stories of their own customers.

During Jobs' second stint with the company, Apple created some of the greatest inventions we've seen in the last hundred years, including the iPod, the iPhone, and the MacBook Pro. This time, Jobs chose to advertise these products through billboards, not newspapers. They would read two simple words: "think different." Jobs had developed a new mission: to recognize the greatness in other people and to give them tools so that they could think differently and achieve greatness through their individuality.

Apple has gone on to become one of the most successful companies in the world and a leader in its industry. It is the company we turn to for the newest trends. When people want to "upgrade" the technology in their own lives, they often think of Apple. More than that, customers have become cult followers of the brand and will buy anything that the company puts out. Apple fans frequently believe that its products help them to grow as people. This culture came about because Steve Jobs learned how to grow, change his ways, and innovate. He both *accepted* and *created* change, rather than resist it.

No Longer Crippled by Fear of Change

I try not to resist change anymore, because I know it'll leave me stuck in a growth trap. When the pandemic hit last year and we were forced to stay in our houses or by ourselves in our workspaces, we began a long period of change. Of course, I was hardly the only one who geared up for a new way of living, nor was I the only one who was scared of the unknown. On top of my concern about the inevitable changes to my personal and professional routines, there was a constant fear in the air, as so many people around the world were in pain and suffering. I felt just like I did in 2008, when I'd faced the most difficult growth trap of my life.

During the chaos that COVID-19 brought, I decided I wasn't going to freeze; I was going to keep moving forward even in this confusing, painful, and turbulent time. My routine changed, my strategy changed, and my plan for the future continued to evolve. And so, I did not get trapped. I'm proud to say that, after years of allowing change to cripple me, by 2020 I'd become adaptable enough to be able to handle novel circumstances.

As I write this book in late 2021, it's clear that the last two years have accelerated a lot of global trends in technology and workplace culture that had already been in motion. Zoom meetings and other virtual technology applications have proven their merit during the pandemic, and they show no signs of being tossed aside anytime soon. This pandemic just sped up the process of the widespread adoption of virtual technology. But did we speed up our own thinking? Did we keep up with the pace of change all around us?

The pandemic forced me to reflect on how I spend my time. At my age and with my familial and professional responsibilities, I realized that I simply had no time to be trapped any longer. Like Steve Jobs, I had to recognize that, if I found myself moving in the wrong direction, I'd need to take the tools around me to change my strategy and become a better, more useful version of myself.

So how exactly did I do that?

One: I now use technology to solve my problems more than ever before. For example, I spend less time in the car and more time meeting new people. By using virtual technologies, I can meet twice as many people a week as I could previously. The meetings also have boundaries, meaning they have a rigorous time limit before the virtual technology ends the meeting automatically. So the open-ended, three-hour lunch meeting has now turned into a tight but efficient one-hour virtual meeting. This allows me to do more in a single day and use my time more productively. As my children grow older, they are busier than they used to be, and if I'm not careful with my time, I can miss out on spending time with them. By streamlining my business and taking advantage of going virtual, I stole back time and have been able to see my children grow more than I did before the pandemic. I have a feeling that I'll look back at 2020–2021 and see it as a pivotal time period in my life, if only because I adapted to the new world and became a better family man as a result.

You don't have to wait for a pandemic to strike in order to improve the processes in your life. How might *you* take more time for yourself and your family?

As technology becomes a greater and greater part of our lives, I will automate more and more and adapt to the changes around me. My processes will become even more efficient, and I'll earn back time to pursue more of what I *want* and less of what I *have* to do.

I believe that what today's buyers and sellers want more than anything is efficient, fast communication and information when they need it. I have come to appreciate the value in delivering a virtual experience that all of my clients will enjoy. Also, tools like e-signing and virtual tours are going to become mandatory for any real estate professional to master. I never would have thought that automation and software technology would have been so important to my growth, but the modern world has amazing technologies to offer. We just have to take advantage of them.

Two: I am adapting to an ever-changing market. In my line of work, the real estate landscape has completely shifted over the last two years. We currently have a lack of homes for sale and an excess demand from people looking to buy homes because they want more space. In the United States, the number of people working remotely has increased by over 40 percent from 2015 to 2020.[6] Furthermore, to many people's surprise, studies have shown that productivity while working remotely is actually higher than while working at an office.[7] The numbers are clear: work-from-home is here to stay. Maybe there will always be office buildings, but more and more of our homes are becoming our workspaces as well. Because of this trend, people want part of their home to be a comfortable, stress-free place where they can work.

Interestingly, virtual tours and remote real estate deals are also on the rise. More than ever, people are buying property without ever stepping foot in the physical property. According to the *New York Times*, "between the second and third quarters of this year [2020], the number of sales listings with 3-D tours increased by 110 percent. And Zillow reported a 152 percent increase in listings with 3-D home tours between this October and the same time last year."[8]

Because of people's preferences for what they want their home to be *and* because many people can now work from any location, I've changed my real estate investing strategy accordingly. For example, I've purchased homes that are in "experience areas" that can be rented for short periods of time through Airbnb, Vrbo, and almost all travel websites. By my definition, experience areas are any residences in close proximity to beaches, lakes, mountains, and tourist attractions. I believe

6   Wong, Kellie. 2020. "25 Key Remote Work Statistics for 2020." Business 2 Community. April 7, 2020. https://www.business2community.com/human-resources/25-key-remote-work-statistics-for-2020-02299342.

7   Apollo Technical. 2020. "Surprising Working from Home Productivity Statistics (2020)." Apollo Technical LLC. September 3, 2020. https://www.apollotechnical.com/working-from-home-productivity-statistics/.

8   Franklin, Sydney. 2020. "Real Estate Transactions Go Virtual." *The New York Times*, November 11, 2020, sec. Real Estate. https://www.nytimes.com/2020/11/11/realestate/10virtual-deals.html.

that the number of people renting these types of spaces for short periods of time to work, live, vacation, and enjoy particular experiences is only going to rise. On the flip side, traditional, long-term rentals will decrease over the coming years. I've embraced these changes and adapted my business plans in order to grow as a professional.

Three: I am going to be more vocal about my beliefs and boundaries. Wasting time around the people who don't have your best interests in mind not only sends you into a growth trap, but it can also cost you years of your life that could've been better spent surrounding yourself with people who would enrich your life.

My experience during the pandemic of riots, racism, and protests has forever changed me. I want to surround myself with positive people who are working on growth and not stuck living in the past. Sometimes, the people in our life treat us as they did when we first met. They refuse to acknowledge that we've grown, and that they should change the way they interact with us. This is why I continue to add people to my circle of growth. I constantly seek out people who recognize me for who I am *now*, accept me, and choose to grow *with* me into the future. I've spent way too much time saying yes to things I didn't want to do, surrounding myself with people whose company I didn't enjoy, and going to places where I didn't need to be. For a long time, I didn't have a strong enough resolve to say no and to take my own boundaries seriously.

Over the next few years, my growth will be highly focused on adjusting my strategies to meet the changes that the pandemic has brought to our world. I also want to lift people up to grow alongside me. I want to teach those people how to avoid the failures that I've made in my life. As I'll talk about in the next chapter, my plan is to launch an academy that will spawn leaders, not followers. I will create more leaders in our society who are armed with knowledge, experience, and a network of mentors. This growth will go both ways—by training the next generation, I will be a better example for my children and other loved ones who need my help in order to grow. Never again will my growth be trapped through ignorance, negative thoughts, and harmful influences.

Takeaways

- If we want to avoid getting trapped by the constant changes of life, we need to become adaptable. A lot of growth traps are caused simply by an irrational resistance to change.
- Even amidst chaos, you need to decide that you won't freeze. Your routines will change, your strategy will change, and your plan for the future will continue to evolve. This way, you will not become trapped by the chaos.
- As I write this book in late 2021, it's clear that the last two years have accelerated a lot of global trends in technology and workplace culture that had already been in motion. Zoom meetings and other virtual technology applications have proven their merit during the pandemic, and they show no signs of being tossed aside anytime soon. This pandemic just sped up the process of the widespread adoption virtual technology. We need to speed up our own thinking in turn.

Chapter Fourteen—

Life in the Now

My seven-year-old son Lucas is an inquisitive boy. He's constantly starved for knowledge and asks so many questions. Honestly, he's the first person who taught me the virtue of patience. Impatience has always been a personal flaw of mine. I've always been impatient with accomplishing my goals, impatient with those around me, impatient with those who couldn't do things I could do, impatient in making a long-term plan and sticking to it. I had grown a bit more patient over the years before having children, but Lucas has helped me focus and become far more patient, which in turn has helped my growth in all sorts of other ways.

My five-year-old daughter Leina is a really happy child, and she looks so much like me. She's always laughing and making jokes. You can just look at her from across the room, and she'll smile, giggle, or scream in response (I've learned that little girls scream a lot). Daily, weekly, and yearly, Leina shows me that life's not so serious—that you should stop and smile and laugh whenever you get a chance.

Every time I look at her, we laugh. It's practically become part of our daily routine.

Both of my children have taught me things that have helped me get out of my growth traps. Yet, I'm *still* in a growth trap. The growth trap is something we deal with for our entire lives. It's something we have to constantly work on. Even though I have implemented all the techniques that I've detailed in this book to get out of the growth trap, I'm still always in a growth trap of one kind or another. I have to learn how to advance every single day and expand my mind to both climb out of current traps and avoid falling back into old traps.

A Tale of Two Tryouts

Recently, Lucas, who has inherited my love of sports, had a baseball tryout for the local travel team. He was so excited to have been invited. On a breezy summer night, the whole family went to watch Lucas try out. He was one boy of seventy pursuing only twelve spots on the team. Lucas was distracted during the entire tryout. It's not really his fault. He's a happy kid. He likes to talk, likes to laugh, and likes to interact with other children. But I knew that if he didn't make the team, he would regret it, and it would hurt him later on in life—old habits die young, after all. Throughout the tryout, Lucas continued to make mistakes because he wasn't paying attention.

I kept calling out to him, "Pay attention! Lucas, focus!" None of it seemed to work. By the end of the tryout, I was so frustrated—he missed his last five pitches when hitting—that I walked away from the tryout and let my wife walk home with him. He didn't even hit one ball because he was so unprepared.

I walked home with Leina, holding her hand and trying to calm myself down. I didn't want to be the father that yelled at his child when I was frustrated with him. By the time he got home, he had realized that he had failed and started to cry. He was upset that he had performed so poorly. As much as it pained me to see him like that, I couldn't show him any sympathy because it would've sent the wrong message.

After we both calmed down, we sat down to have a conversation. I said to him, "This is going to keep happening if you don't pay attention and don't try hard." I explained to him that to get what he wants, he is going to have to focus more, work hard, and practice. I told Lucas that he didn't *have* to do any of this—he could just be happy playing on a regular baseball team, going out, and having fun with his friends. I would have been completely fine with that.

"I don't want you to do it for me," I said to him. "But if you want it, it's going to take work."

There was one more tryout the following week. He was not supposed to be there because our whole family was supposed to be away for a three-day weekend at the Jersey shore. I asked Lucas if he wanted to try out again. He looked up at me with innocent but determined eyes and said yes.

"Okay," I said. "We're going to have to practice this whole week, and when I'm not here, you're going to have to practice on your own. And when we get to the tryout, you're going to have to pay attention, focus, and try your hardest. If trying your hardest doesn't work and you don't make the team, then we'll do something else, no big deal. As long as you try hard and work at it, there's nothing else you can do."

Lucas and I practiced the whole weekend. We went to the batting cages and played catch, and we did it with enthusiasm. During the following week, he heeded my advice and practiced while I wasn't there.

We drove for over two hours from the shore to get to the tryout on a Friday night. Lucas hit the field with complete focus and played very well. I was so proud of him for trying hard and not fooling around or letting himself get distracted.

At the end of the tryout, the coaches announced that there would be a water slide for all of the kids who played in the tryouts. While most of the kids who stayed around ran to the water slide, Lucas stayed back and approached one of the coaches to ask if he could show him how to pitch from the pitcher's mound. I was completely blown away. He could've hit five homeruns, and it wouldn't have made me prouder than this moment. He wanted to learn for learning's sake, just to better himself. I watched him try as hard as he could to throw from the pitcher's mound for ten minutes straight. When he came back, I told him that whether or not he made the team, he tried his best, and that I'd always be proud of him for that moment.

Later on that week, Lucas was chosen as one of twelve children to make the team. Honestly, I was surprised, but I couldn't have been happier for my son.

The truth is that this was more of a learning and growth moment for me than it was for him. Lucas showed me once again that I needed to grow, that I needed to be more patient with him. I learned to gauge his emotions more accurately and to teach him that it's not necessarily about wins and losses, but about not having regrets that we didn't do our best when we really wanted to. Giving such a patient explanation does not come naturally to me. After that first tryout, I was so frustrated that I wanted to yell at him that I'd never take him to the baseball field again. Instead, he taught me to be patient and to work harder to do the right thing. Lucas and I both learned that, in the end, we'd continue to be successful if we put our best foot forward. This was another moment of growth out of my trap that I struggle with to this day: be patient, trust the process, and press onward.

The Generation Disruptor Scholarship Program

I am writing these pages in 2021. One year earlier, our country was in the grips of the COVID-19 pandemic. This was a terrible time when people were getting sick and dying, and millions more were out of work and despairing. On top of that, we were in the perils of racial and governmental strife that, because people were cooped up in their houses for so long, was ready to burst.

Living and working around New York City, I saw the anger first-hand. Early in the summer of 2020, I witnessed protests and demonstrations against a myriad of problems. In some cases, I sympathized with the protestors, but along with the protests came rioting and looting. Every morning, I would wake up and immediately turn on the news, which is unusual for me. It's against everything I preach. I never watch the news because it's too negative. But watching the city that I grew up in and love being torn apart really upset me. It wasn't just the stores being looted and their windows being smashed that bothered me. It was the despair and the lost look in people's eyes—they had no idea where to go or how to help.

People became even more enraged when George Floyd was senselessly killed by police officers. All the anger and frustration about race and police brutality exploded across the nation.

My own family is of mixed race. My wife, Beatriz, was born in the Dominican Republic and immigrated here when she was a young girl. She has a huge family, and we have a lot of fun mixing our ethnic cultures together. It's always been a source of pride to me that we came from different backgrounds but made it work regardless.

Beyond my own family, I have a wide variety of friends. I've always been enamored with different races and cultures. Since I was a little boy, I've always loved learning about other people: where they came from, what made them different, and how I could learn more and improve my own life by learning from them.

Event for Generation Disruptor scholarship

Initial Generation Disruptor Scholarship class

I've witnessed racism around me my whole life. People think that, because I'm a white male, it's okay to say racist things to me. This has always made me really uncomfortable. When this happens, I usually just look at the person, don't say anything, and walk away. On the other hand, I've also experienced incidents where I've argued and even gotten into physical altercations.

But during the protests of 2020, I asked myself, "What have I ever really done to change things?"

Sure, I wasn't perpetuating any stereotypes or racism, but what was I doing to change things or stop it? I decided that I wasn't doing enough. I couldn't just act the right way in my own life. I wanted to, needed to help change things so that my children wouldn't grow up being looked at the wrong way or treated differently depending on whether they were "passing" as white or perceived as mixed race.

One day, after another episode of rioting and looting the night before, I hopped in my car first thing in the morning with garbage bags and a broom. Out of sheer frustration, I headed to the Bronx by myself. I drove up and down the street, looking at smashed windows and people crying because their homes and stores had been destroyed and robbed. I needed to do something. I saw one particular store where the glass had been smashed and the inside had been completely emptied. I got out of my car with my broom and garbage bags and started cleaning up. A friend joined me, and for two hours we helped the family put the store back together as best we could. I packed up my things, returned home, and prepared to go to work. Good deed done for the day.

But I still felt completely empty. This wasn't enough. All of the marching and protesting, even if it was peaceful and helped get the people's voices out, wasn't enough. I needed to do more, to help people grow as empowered individuals.

As I stated early on in this chapter, my children teach me new things every day. They've also given me a new perspective on my responsibility as a person they can follow, look up to, and learn life lessons from. This gives me a reason to grow every day and not be trapped. Your motivation doesn't have to be your children, or your significant other, or your parents. You could just want to be better for the people who will come after you. I am motivated to be better, not just for my children, but for the people who work underneath me, and for all the people who watch me from a distance through my social media. And I also need to be a good person when no one is looking. I need to teach others through my past and current mistakes.

This was one of those moments when I had to be better. I had to figure out how I could impact other people.

Enter the Generation Disruptor Scholarship Program.

I did not believe that my time would be best spent by protesting and posting on social media about the problems we were facing. I knew that, through my connections and knowledge, I could help in a different way. The best thing I could do was to give people who hadn't had access to opportunities the ability to take advantage of my knowledge and my network and to learn skills that would help them better their own lives and their family's situation. I decided to create a scholarship to help youths who needed insight and the opportunity to obtain licensing in mortgages and/or real estate. I could help them become either loan officers or real estate agents. They could then pursue this profession that would be fruitful for decades to come. Even if it wasn't something they wanted to do as a job for the rest of their lives, the scholarship experience would educate them on the process of how to buy real estate, how to invest in themselves, and how to obtain a license as a mortgage, financial, and/or real estate professional.

When I created a scholarship, I didn't have much of a plan. I was just desperate to relieve some of the stress in my brain about the current environment. One of the first things I did was set up criteria for choosing scholars. I wanted each applicant to be under twenty-five, have a genuine interest in real estate, and be hungry and driven. I also wanted to choose applicants who lacked their own access to the type of business I was involved in.

We put the contest out on social media, on community college and vocational school message boards, and in local churches and community centers. My plan was to hire four individuals and give them a paid internship for ninety days. If they were able to complete the internship, I would pay for their licensing in their field of choice. The instructors would be my immediate team and me, with some help from a few outside realtors and loan officers who would give them field experience.

We put the criteria up and received hundreds of inquiries within ten days. I then conducted phone interviews with about ten applicants that my team had narrowed the applicant pool down to. Through those interviews, we chose four people. And so it began.

On the first day, they were all excited and nervous. Truthfully, I was probably more nervous than the scholars were. What had I just taken on? How would I fit this into my schedule? How could I even make an impact?

In the next few months, we taught them the basic skills of both mortgage and real estate, specific phone and writing skills for these industries, social media presence and structure, what my investment portfolio consisted of and how it has been shaped through failing and practicing, and basic interaction skills in how to professionally handle other people's finances. They also shadowed my colleagues and me in order to gain firsthand experience and to figure out for themselves which aspects of the business they were most passionate about.

It was an amazing and challenging experience. Besides trying to teach them basic skills in ninety days that took me years to master—ninety days wasn't enough time, it turned out—there were also generational and philosophical differences between how I learned my skills and how modern young people prefer to learn. When I received multiple paid-time-off requests during this short, paid internship, my head almost exploded. The internship that I had offered them didn't even exist when I was their age, so I was confused why they preferred time off over valuable experience. When I was in my twenties, I didn't even know what paid time off was! I was always someone who earned strictly on commission and, later, on the profits of my business. I hadn't had a job in which I was paid by the hour since I made minimum wage as a teenager working at a sneaker store. Also, when I first started out in my business, someone at my current level never even said hello to me, never mind spending forty hours a week with me and then paying me for it! But this was a different time, which I discovered thanks to these four individuals. Once again, I learned to be more patient. I came to understand the difference between my mind-set and theirs. As a result, I changed the way I interacted with them so that they could better understand what it took for me to get where I am.

By the end of the program, all four interns had earned positions in my organization. They had also improved their philosophies and learned new skills that made them deserving of full-time jobs no matter what path they might go on to take. Since that time, three of the interns are still employed by me. As of writing this, three of the four interns have been licensed, and all four remain in the business. They continue to progress, since they are willing to adapt to their environment without their ego getting in the way. They took full advantage of the access I gave them and used it to start their businesses, which will enable them to help those who come after them.

Some of my interns told me that there weren't any opportunities like the one I'd offered them in their home communities. "There were no places where I could build myself or get an apprenticeship," one of them told me. "There was no place where I could grow and learn about a field and take care of my family."

I learned a lot about my own growth traps, too. It turns out that no matter how experienced I am in my own field, *teaching* others is an entirely new ball game! Starting fresh is always a little intimidating, but if you think about all of the possibilities that can come of your new project, you will have a much easier time adapting and thriving. This was exactly what happened when I took on my first batch of interns.

My ultimate goal is to have an academy full of these disruptors. Since my first round of interns in August 2020, I have taken on four more hires under a similar model. My mission with the Disruptors Academy is to create more leaders, rather than more followers. Something of a slogan for the academy that I mostly keep to myself is, "A new team, a new society." How many more businesses will we create in underserved communities because of our Disruptors Academy in the next three, five, ten years? I don't know, but I'm excited to find out.

When No One is Watching

I learned another unexpected and valuable lesson through this program. It's not enough for me not to be racist or discriminating. It's not enough to be a good person who speaks out in a comfortable circle but never to the masses of strangers who feel differently than I do. I have to be stronger and more vocal, even when it's challenging and uncomfortable. I still believe that we can be anything we choose to be, that no obstacle of discrimination can stop us if we really want something. But I have to be open-minded enough to understand other people's plights so that I can help them.

Every day, I ask myself a very intimate and crucial question: who are you when no one is looking? If I'm being honest, I've done things when I was by myself that would embarrass me if others saw. But just because no one knows that I did something wrong doesn't make me feel any better about my choice. It's actually *worse*, because then I'm trapped with thoughts of guilt and embarrassment. It has happened before and it could happen again, but my growth will not be trapped by it. As long as I am able, I will continue to become better all the time. I will strive to act as if the world is watching me.

I've also realized that not everyone is going to like me or agree with me, no matter what I do. My Instagram account, @dibug, is a big way by which I spread my message to the world. I try my best to be as transparent as I can, to show who I really am on my journey. Some people like me for my inspiration, and some people don't like me for whatever reason. They unfollow me, talk badly about me behind my back, and in general have a negative attitude toward my mission and my voice. I have to be okay with that, because I'm okay with who I truly am. The only person we have to be comfortable with is ourselves.

Who are we when no one else is watching? As long as I can look at myself in the mirror and see a fulfilled person, then I will continue to grow every day and do my best to never be trapped again. Staying out of the growth trap does not just mean becoming more successful in business. It also means raising your own social consciousness, progressing along with society and learning to see things in a new way.

Takeaways

- Children can help you escape out of your growth trap in ways you could never have imagined.
- You should stop and smile and laugh whenever you get a chance.

- Who are you when no one is looking? We've all done things when we were by ourselves that would embarrass us if others saw. It happened before and it could happen again, but your growth should not be trapped by it. As long as you are able, you should continue to become better all the time. You should strive to act as if the world is watching you.

Chapter Fifteen–
Conclusion: The End of the Beginning

We've come a long way. Throughout this book, we've discussed the nature of the growth trap: its different shapes and sizes, the conditions under which you might fall into one, strategies to climb out of it, and real examples of people falling into and then escaping it. We've also journeyed through much of my own story and many of my personal battles with various growth traps.

It's natural to forget the lessons you've discovered in a book long after you've finished it. If you find yourself stuck in a growth trap years after having read this book, I don't want you to feel like you'd have to reread every chapter to find the solution to your problem. In that spirit, I want to give you a quick overview of some of the lessons we've explored in the previous pages. If you ever need guidance on how to escape the growth trap but don't have time to reread the entire book, *this* is where you should come to.

1. **Growth traps come in many forms.**

People suffer through adolescent growth traps, social growth traps, romantic growth traps, physical growth traps, and professional growth traps. Some types of growth traps are unique to *groups* of people, rather than individuals. For example, companies may fall into a stagnating pattern that they need to climb out of if they want to remain competitive.

2. **Growth traps are inevitable.**

Once you begin to implement your growth plan, don't be afraid to make adjustments along the way. In fact, mistakes are inevitable on the path to improvement. Most great leaders suffer many losses during their lifetimes. The key is to recognize when your growth plan is not working and to make changes before mistakes begin to compound. Replace ego with self-critical discipline, and you won't have any trouble modifying your growth plan.

3. **Don't let your expert blinders stop you from thinking like a beginner.**

When we think like an expert, we tend to let our egos get in our own way. But as children, we'll do anything, try anything without hesitation or fear. As children, we're always thinking like beginners. We all remember what it was like to let our imagination roam free. The most successful adults retain that youthful, ego-free imagination. They don't shackle their own potential with the arrogant, static mind-set of thinking like an expert. The good news is that, no matter your age, you can always return to the beginner's mind-set. Don't let your potential suffocate under the weight of expert blinders. Instead, think like a beginner, and rediscover the fun of growing.

4. **Be intentional about growing.**

Intentional growth is made much easier if you first develop a plan for yourself. Figure out which daily, incremental steps you need to execute in order to improve. Mistakes are inevitable, but how you react is not. Instead of giving up or letting frustration control you, make adjustments to your plan so that you can turn the ship around and continue to intentionally grow. The most fundamental requirement to grow intentionally is to get up every day and improve over who you were yesterday. Never allow yourself to "cruise" from one day to the next.

5. **Develop a plan for how you will escape the growth trap.**

We are never going to feel ready to grow. We are never going to feel fully equipped to implement our plan and escape the growth trap. Still, that doesn't justify never starting. To take action, we have to first decide what our goal is, then establish a long-term plan in order to achieve it, and finally move toward that goal over time. As we act on that plan, we will have short-term setbacks, failures, and moments of doubt. We may even lose faith that we can reach the goal at all. All of this is normal. During your long-term plan, don't be afraid to pivot and make adjustments if something isn't working. I went from planning a Mastermind class to hosting a two-hundred-person live event, and it was one of the best professional decisions I'd ever made. Figure out how to leverage your network in order to execute your plan.

6. **Comfort leads to stagnation.**

Pursuing only goals that are easy to accomplish is one of the greatest obstacles to growth. I guarantee that no effortless task will produce any personal growth or progress. The hard road, on the other hand, forces us to grow. The hard road will make us better every single day that we choose to go down it.

7. **Sometimes, you have no choice but to force growth.**

Stop giving yourself excuses like, "I just need to wait until the time is right." At some point, we have to look in the mirror and decide to force growth with intention, full stop. At times, this will be painful, but we need to ignore the short-term pain and focus on our long-term goals in order to get to where we want to be.

There is no such thing as a transition. Growth comes from putting your back against the wall and figuring out a plan to force growth. To me, transition has always meant doing something with half effort. No great result will come without your best effort toward your long-term goal. The longer of a "transition phase" you grant yourself, the more you delay your best years of growth.

8. **Pain can be a catalyst for fostering a growth mind-set.**

Look at each event as a test. Bad events can happen to anyone. I don't believe things happen *to* us, but rather *for* us. Painful events can be interpreted as life lessons that we can use moving forward. No matter what kind of particular pain we've suffered, we can learn from it by mining it for life lessons. Painful events and/or failure can be empowering, if only we use them in the right way. Success never comes easy. Always take a bad experience and turn it into a positive.

The darkest times can be the greatest opportunities for growth. My darkest times in life were when I was the most broke, the most hurt, and the most emotionally starved. They have all served as empowering moments for me later in life. I turn to them every time I'm struggling or stressed. During these times, I tell myself, "If I made it through *that* painful experience of the past, I can make it through anything." Take responsibility and embrace the pain. Blaming others will never help you make progress. Looking to others for blame isn't going to fix the problem or the pain, and it won't make us better. Instead, we can respond positively to our pain in order to ensure that we don't end up suffering from the same kind of pain down the road.

9. Get comfortable failing.

Mistakes are a sign that we're actively working toward a win. This is one reason why it's okay to fail. In fact, it's actually your mission to fail. Times of failure are when you will learn all of the lessons that you'll need to eventually succeed. No one wins all of the time, no one reaches greatness by protecting themselves from losses. It is the losses that make you strong enough to do things you never thought you could.

The most common mistake that young entrepreneurs make is becoming or wanting to become the person at the front of the room before you are ready. It's perfectly fine to work for someone else for a while and learn from them before venturing out on your own.

10. Your network is an undervalued asset.

Before you pursue your long-term goal, write down who you have in your network that can be an asset in making sure the relevant tasks get done. Also, reach out to those who have experience and/or could serve as advisors toward your goals. During lengthy projects, you'll need people around you who carry a positive attitude and can be transparent with you regarding whether or not your initial plans seem to be taking you toward your long-term goal.

Another key to a long-term plan is for the network that you leverage to be consistent, predictable, and reliable. If you can understand where your people will be and how they will respond and if you can rely on them to respond as you would, you will enjoy the peace and security necessary to focus on your plan.

11. Learn to pivot fast when your plan is not panning out.

When your business takes a financial hit or when projects fail—and they will—the most important thing you can do is move forward, stay consistent, and find a quick solution. Standing still will never, ever get your business where it needs to be. As an entrepreneur, you will need to pivot fast and often. Failure is not a death sentence, it's fuel for business and personal growth.

One kind of growth trap is getting stuck in a rut of daily efforts that, while they may be effective, are taking us down the wrong path. To honestly analyze whether or not we are on the right path, we need to ask ourselves a few questions about where our talents, passions, and potential lie.

12. The difference between success and failure is the quality of your habits.

Why is it sometimes helpful to have our back up against the wall in order to form new habits? If making my high school basketball team was a do-or-die scenario, I guarantee that I would've figured out how to make it. This tells us that changing our habits is ultimately a mind-set issue. Mentally, if we stop giving ourselves the option of quitting or not changing our habits, then we give ourselves an opportunity to grow.

Routines create a predictable structure for my life: I get up and know that some of my tasks are exactly the same every day. This consistency alone takes a lot of life's pressures off the table. *That* is the beauty of habits.

13. The four foundational principles of habit formation.

There are four foundational principles of habit formation.

First, we all go through short-term pain to reach our long-term goal. The key is to create your long-term goal with a focus on incremental growth *toward* that goal.

Second, add the right accountability partners to your circle. To create good habits and routines, you might need some help. Whatever your goal is, you can find a way to keep yourself accountable through other people.

Third, ignore what others are doing. In a world of social media and constant comparisons, we look at our peers and judge them over how well or badly they're doing. The simple truth is that you just need to concentrate on how *you're* doing.

Fourth, surround yourself with positive energy. Outside of accountability partners, we need positive people and influences around us. This applies to our daily routines as much as to any other part of our lives. For example, you could be spending too much time with a family member or friend who always complains or discourages you. Your growth has no time for such influences. Find people who make you want to be better, get up, do more, and innovate. Surround yourself with people who motivate you toward your long-term goals and encourage you to establish better habits.

14. **Learn to operate in the present moment.**

When we use our past experiences to solve problems in our present, we are progressing and avoiding the growth trap. When we feel the need to talk about our past accomplishments because they are more impressive than what we are doing today, we are holding onto something that is inhibiting our ability to make progress.

Obsessing with the future can also be debilitating as a mental process. If your mental process includes thoughts like "I will get to it" or "I will do it tomorrow" with no action plan, you will continue to disappoint yourself over and over. Comfort and fear will keep us stuck in whatever we are currently doing forever, unless we turn desire for change into action. I know it can be scary to go out and do what's necessary to change, but you must accept that progress is rarely easy to achieve. Some people are stuck in a job, relationship, or mind-set because of the sheer fear of what's next—the future. Predictions of the future without a plan of action can be our greatest copout and the largest reason why we remain stuck.

15. The six-month plan.

To take action, we have to first decide what our goal is, then establish a long-term plan in order to achieve it, and finally move toward that goal over time. As we act on that plan, we will have short-term setbacks, failures, and moments of doubt. We may even lose faith that we can reach our goal at all. All of this is normal. Such feelings are part of the process that is our long-term plan. The long-term plan is a repeatable strategy that is imperative for avoiding the growth trap and advancing forward, like a recipe that yields good results every time—if you stick to it.

What has worked for me throughout my career is creating a six-month plan. It's not so long that my daily, weekly, and monthly schedule are negatively impacted, and it's not so short that small setbacks and failures will compromise the mission. To make a long-term plan successful, we need to learn what works and what doesn't, and adjust accordingly as we grow toward success.

16. Choosing to fight rather than run away.

Fight-or-flee is that thought in your mind right before you confront something that's scaring you. You make a quick decision to attack or run. This instinct doesn't only kick in when you're facing a literal fight. Anything could trigger a fight-or-flee response. It could be something as harmless as writing down your thoughts, which might terrify you. It could be continuing to run down the road, even when you're out of breath.

Most people will never admit this, but fear dominates their lives. Fear of loss. Fear of failure. Fear of being alone. Fear of never succeeding. Living in a constant state of "flee" will never get us anywhere we want to go. To avoid getting caught in the growth trap of "flee," you have to learn to accept fear and fight through it.

17. The anatomy of a great comeback.

This is the anatomy of a great comeback: caught in the growth trap, not reaching our potential, unhappy, and stuck, we decide to make a drastic change, take a chance on ourselves, force growth, and begin a comeback. Our comebacks may not make us famous, but they are essential for reaching our true potential and finding joy in what we do daily.

Every day is a chance to grow, come back, and improve. I have witnessed millions of comeback stories from both watching the news and from the people in my personal life. Sometimes they inspire and amaze us. Sometimes, you might harbor ill will or harsh judgments about the person who made a comeback. That feeling is usually more about your own path than about the person who just came back. The same applies when others judge *you* for *your* success. What we are experiencing is a very superficial kind of hate, but the reality is that your detractors feel insecure and unaccomplished themselves, so they need to diminish your shine to rationalize their lack of it.

18. Become adaptable.

If we want to avoid getting trapped by the constant changes of life, we need to become adaptable. I used to resist change. The mere thought of it gave me intense anxiety, and so I'd avoid it at all costs. Looking back, a lot of my growth traps were caused simply by my irrational resistance to change.

19. **Think about the person you want to be when no one is watching.**

Every day, you should ask yourself a very intimate and crucial question: who are you when no one is looking? If we're being honest, we've all done things when we were by ourselves that would embarrass us if others saw. But just because no one knows that we did something wrong doesn't make us feel any better about our choices. It's actually *worse*, because then we're trapped with thoughts of guilt and embarrassment. It happened before and it could happen again, but our growth does not need to be trapped by it. As long as we am able, we should continue to become better all the time. We should strive to act as if the world is watching us.

Growth traps are all around us, and we will face them every day of our lives. No one can avoid them totally. We will take steps backward sometimes, but by instilling the principles that I've laid out in this book into your routines, you will be able to move forward no matter what stands in your way. I've committed to taking one step forward every day of my life, and I've reaped the reward. That's not to say I don't sometimes take five steps backward for one reason or another—growth traps have a way of snagging even the most disciplined people.

I hope that anyone reading this book is able to move forward at least one more step today because of the stories I've told, the failures I've gone through, and my consistent goal to strive for growth. I am confident that by the time you've reached this chapter, you'll have learned about the tools you can use to become a better person in some way, shape, or form. Personally, I will continue to grow, be transparent about my failures, and never cease to work on becoming a better me. I appreciate all the time you took to learn about my growth process. I hope we can grow together for the rest of our lives.

About the author

R alph DiBugnara is a successful serial entrepreneur and real estate expert. After growing up struggling financially, Ralph knew he wanted more for himself, he didn't want generational poverty to be his future, he wanted to make a generational change. Now he holds the prestigious roles of President of Home Qualified, a digital resource for buyers and sellers, and Vice President at Cardinal Financial, a nationally recognized mortgage loan company. He is even a nationally recognized mortgage banker and real estate, expert. His expertise led him to start a series called The Real Estate Disruptors, where he interviews guests on investing, property guidance, and advice. His program focuses on creating an elite network of industry leaders to help brokers succeed in the social media-driven economy. In addition, Ralph launched a mentoring program for inner-city young adults called "The Generation Disruptor Scholarship Program," developed to educate students on how to get into the real estate industry, break generational curses, and cultivate leaders in their communities. In 2021 Ralph plans on reaching more young adults to help get them into The Generation Disruptor Scholarship Program and start a new future for themselves.

Bibliography

"A Simple Way to Break a Bad Habit | Judson Brewer." n.d. Www. youtube.com. Accessed February 25, 2022. https://www. youtube.com/watch?v=-moW9jvvMr4&t=288s.

Apollo Technical. 2020. "Surprising Working from Home Productivity Statistics (2020)." Apollo Technical LLC. September 3, 2020. https://www.apollotechnical.com/working-from-home-productivity-statistics/.

"Definition of Fear | Dictionary.com." 2016. Www.dictionary.com. 2016. https://www.dictionary.com/browse/fear.

https://disruptnow.org/#:~:text=Disruption% 20% E2% 80% 93% 20Disrupt% 20% 28v% 29% 20% 3A% 20to% 20interrupt% 20% 28an,drastically% 20alter% 20or% 20destroy% 20the% 20structure% 20of% 20% 28something% 29

Franklin, Sydney. 2020. "Real Estate Transactions Go Virtual." *The New York Times*, November 11, 2020, sec. Real Estate. https:// www.nytimes.com/2020/11/11/realestate/10virtual-deals.html.

"Understanding the Stress Response." 2011. Harvard Health. March 1, 2011. https://www.health.harvard.edu/staying-healthy/understanding-the-stress-response#:~:text=A%.

Wong, Kellie. 2020. "25 Key Remote Work Statistics for 2020." Business 2 Community. April 7, 2020. https://www.business2community.com/human-resources/25-key-remote-work-statistics-for-2020-02299342.

"You're Already Awesome. Just Get out of Your Own Way!: Judson Brewer MD, Ph.D. At TEDxRockCreekPark." n.d. Www.youtube.com. Accessed February 25, 2022. https://www.youtube.com/watch?v=jE1j5Om7g0U.

A free ebook edition is available with the purchase of this book.

To claim your free ebook edition:

1. Visit MorganJamesBOGO.com
2. Sign your name CLEARLY in the space
3. Complete the form and submit a photo of the entire copyright page
4. You or your friend can download the ebook to your preferred device

Print & Digital Together Forever.

Snap a photo

Free ebook

Read anywhere